ABOUT DUST FROM
A RED DIRT ROAD

"Terry Freeman's Dust From a Red Dirt Road is so much more than a memoir. It is that, but it's also a personal history of the South, sometimes reaching all the way back to the 17th century. As I read it, I was reminded of Georgia humorist Lewis Grizzard, even before he was mentioned in the book. With belly-laugh-inducing true stories, interspersed with pensive poetry and mouth-watering family recipes, there's something for everyone. The juxtaposition of prose, poetry and recipes gives a picture of life in the South that would be incomplete if each was presented by itself. Even if Freeman's readers aren't from the South, they will appreciate the recurring themes of family, faith, and food, plus the importance of work ethic and community. Freeman writes from the perspective of a family who lived on the same ground for generations, something that is rare and precious today, revealing values that are sorely needed and not to be discarded as old-fashioned. Dust From a Red Dirt Road is a gift from a man who has lived long enough to have thought deeply about life's important questions, but he relates his insightful gems with an impish twinkle in his eye."

Gary L Ivey, Author, Pastor, Award winning screenwriter, Composer

"Dust From a Red Dirt Road" is a joy ride. If you don't know, red dust settles into the slightest crack or crevice. In this book it finds its way deeper into our lives. It settles in the folds of our hearts. And it opens the unforgettable memories in the file cabinet of our minds. In this marvelous book of stories, memories, poetry, and family recipes, master storyteller Terry Freeman dusts our hearts and the memories come alive again. I enjoyed each page and story, just as you will too. But, when you finish, go wash your hands. They'll be covered with red dust."

Joey Hancock, Comedian, Award winning author, Member, Atlanta Country Music Hall of Fame

"I have known Terry for a long time. He's one of the funniest people I've every known. As you read Dust From a Red Dirt Road you'll see that sense of humor. You'll also see a deeper side that very few people see. I highly recommend this book."

Bob Bramblett, USMC (retired), friend, and golf partner

"Terry may not be right all the time, but he always calls it like he sees it. Pay close attention to the chapters *"I Grew Up in the Eastern Shadows of Stone Mountain"* and *"I've Been to the Promised Land."* Great book Cuz!

Thomas Livsey Sr, Civil Rights Activist, "Mayor of the Promised Land"

DUST FROM A RED DIRT ROAD

*Stories, Essays, and Poems from a
Georgia Life...and some Recipes too.*

Terry R Freeman

Tóg bog é Publishing, Snellville, GA 30039

Copyright © 2023 Terry R Freeman

I have tried to recreate events, locales, and conversations from my memories of them. To protect privacy, in some instances I have changed the names of individuals and places, I may have changed some identifying characteristics and details such as physical properties, occupations and places of residence, or not...

https://selfpubbookcovers.com/Cover2Book

Printed in the United States of America

Dedication

This book is dedicated to four people: my wife Judy, my son Nate, and my Mom and Dad.

My precious wife Judy has always believed in me even when I didn't believe in myself.

My son Nate, he has always encouraged me. He continues to be a constant source of joy and pride in my life.

My Mom, Molly Attaway Freeman, was a force of nature. She was the first liberated woman I ever knew.

My Dad, Nathaniel Morris Freeman, was the rock of our family. His example of how to live is the one I follow today. How am I doing Pop?

I love you all.

Terry R. Freeman
December, 2023

CONTENTS

A BRIEF HISTORY OF MY CENTERVILLE HOME

I thought I'd begin this book with a brief history of the community of Centerville, the one in Gwinnett County, Georgia. I was raised here, and still live on the family property, or what's left of it. The following is my completely biased attempt at said history.

An early 1950's photograph of downtown Centerville.

Let's start with the indigenous people, or native people, or as our Canadian friends call them "The First Nations." I'll use the term "Indian" for clarity and continuity, and it's easier to type. The Indian history of the Centerville area is a long one. They were here at least 8 to 10 thousand years before Columbus. At first, wandering hunter-gatherers came through. They were usually in groups of 25 to 50 and followed the streams and rivers. With the development of agriculture, groups became larger. These large groups became what we now call tribes. Agriculture brought towns. There were many towns in what became Gwinnett County. All these towns were on or near a river or stream. The largest town was north of Centerville, near the Chattahoochee. Before the Cherokee came around 1700 this was a Creek town. Sometime, again pre-Cherokee, a large group of Shawnee settled there. So many, in fact, it was known as Shawnee Old Town. Today it's called Suwanee.

One thing leads to another. Towns led to trade, and trade begat trails. Here's some the trails that pass through, or near Centerville: Hightower, Sandtown, Peachtree, and good old Rockbridge. Rockbridge is a spur trail that connects the Hightower to the Peachtree. It follows the route of GA 124 through Centerville. Now, about the Peachtree trail. Some folks claim that "Peachtree" is a corruption of "pitch tree." This supposedly refers to the abundant pine trees that produce pitch. I call Bullfeathers. This argument didn't appear until the

20th Century. "Standing Peachtree" was the name of a Creek village and can be traced back to the 18th century. It appears on a document from 1782. Bull feathers indeed.

Back to our Rockbridge trail. As I said earlier, it's a spur trail that runs off the Hightower in a northeasterly direction. It was known as the Rock Bridge Trail because of a granite shelf that makes the Yellow River fordable most of the year. In the late 1600's, when Europeans first saw the Rock Bridge they asked the Creeks, "Who made this trail?" The native people told them the trails were there when they got there. They said the "ancient ones" made them.

Not too far from Centerville is the big rock, Stone Mountain (more about Stone Mountain in the chapter *I Was Raised in the Eastern Shadows of Stone Mountain*.) In response to the increasing threat of European intrusion, surviving tribes formed alliances during the late eighteenth century. These became known as the Creek Confederation. Stone Mountain lay between the Creek Confederation and the Cherokee nation. The mountain, that had always been sacred to both tribes, now became an important meeting place. Two major trails, the Hightower, and the Sandtown connected it to the eastern part of the state.

Creek and Cherokee both lived in this area, not to mention other Indians all the way back to the Archaic period. The first

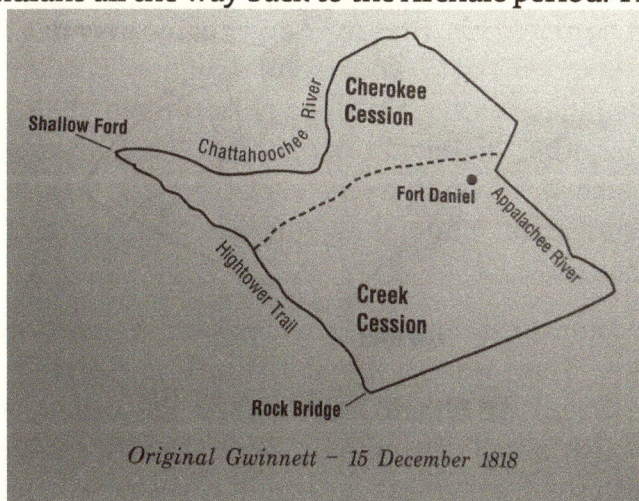

Original Gwinnett – 15 December 1818

treaty that brought land into what became Gwinnett County was signed in 1790 with the Creeks. The last treaty involving soon to be Gwinnett County was signed in 1817. That one was with the Cherokee. Europeans settled illegally near the Rock Bridge, on what was then Indian land, as early as 1810. This "invasion" led to the various treaties that created the county in 1818. The surveyors went to work, and by 1820 the land was marked off and ready to be distributed. The method of distribution was a lottery. The Gwinnet lottery began in September 1820 and ran through December of that year. This 1820 lottery dispensed land that was ceded by the Cherokee in the north, and the Creeks in the south. Centerville is in the Rockbridge District, which is in the southern part, on land that belonged to the Creek Nation.

We'll meet Thomas McGuire again in a later chapter. He arrived in Savannah from Ireland in 1818. He acquired his first property with the lottery of 1820. His lot was fractional, 50 acres, and bordered the Hightower Trail on its southeastern side. With the discovery of gold in Dahlonega and San Francisco and the presence of the terrible boll weevil that destroyed the cotton crops, some of his neighbors got gold fever and left. This allowed Mr. Maguire to buy three parcels of land that bordered his. His estate eventually grew to 956 acres. Maguire married David Anderson's daughter Jane Anderson. Following Jane's death from blood poisoning in 1837, Maguire married another of David's daughters, Elizabeth. Maguire is remembered for farm diary he kept from 1859 to 1866. For information about Thomas Maguire see the chapter, *I've Been to the Promised Land.*

Another pioneer family of the Centerville area were the Andersons. They were originally from Cumberland County Virginia. Elijah Anderson built a farm he called "Pleasant Valley." It consisted of a church, general store, cabinet shop, blacksmith shop, cotton gin, grist mill, and sawmill. Elijah had a brother, David. David and his wife, Mourning, had 6 children. Unfortunately, David was killed during the War of 1812. The two oldest girls, Jane, and Elizabeth came to live with their Uncle Elijah and Aunt Celia. They raised the girls as their own. That's how they came to be in Centerville, and thus met and married Thomas Maguire.

Slavery. That disgusting institution that still haunts us today. Slavery is like a scar on America's skin. A scar that tears every time she moves. All the early settlers we've met were slaveholders. I won't sugarcoat that, nor will I dwell on it.

Centerville was simply known as Rockbridge in its earliest days. Before the Civil War folks started calling it Sneezer. Why Sneezer? No one knows. When the post office was established in 1879, Sneezer became Centerville. The first postmaster was

Tyrannus Judson Minor. His friends called him T J. He served 6 years. He was succeeded by Mr. J.L. Evans in 1885. Mr. Evans served until the post office was closed.in 1903.

Dr. James M. Guess was born in Stone Mountain in 1853. He graduated from the Medical College of Georgia in 1878 and returned home and established his practice. Dr. Guess was one of the earliest physicians in DeKalb County. He also saw patients in Centerville for many years. Sadly, he died of a cerebral hemorrhage in 1915 at the age of 61.

Centerville prospered and had a couple of general stores. One of the stores was owned by James Emory Freeman. He was Hamilton Franklin Freeman's son. When my great grandfather, AD Freeman was killed, Papa Freeman, two of his brothers, and his stepmother Ellen appointed the administrator of AD's estate on a piece of paper from the store.

AD Freeman Estate Administrator
Appointment

Several county and state officials were born and raised in Centerville. Benjamin P. Weaver was described by Gwinnett County Historian, James C. Flannigan, as a "popular man with great ability." Mr. Weaver was a Captain in the 42nd Georgia Volunteer Infantry, Company B. He was killed in 1864 at the Battle of Franklin, Tennessee. Mr. Harold J. Campbell was the county tax collector. Mr. James Palmer Mason was county sheriff from 1936 to 1940. Mr. Everett Ezra Norton was tax receiver. In more recent times the late Jimmy Mason and his brother Wayne Mason have served in county and state offices.

Last, that I can remember, is Centerville native Dan Curry. Dan has served as city councilman and mayor of the city of Loganville. He also spearheaded the Centerville History Group for the Gwinnett County Bicentennial in 2018. I'm sure I've missed some folks, but it's not intentional.

Centerville, for the longest time, had only 2 churches; Zoar Methodist and Rockbridge Baptist. Zoar was organized long before the Civil War, some say in 1811, but the actual date is unknown. Zoar's first building was on Clower (now Everson) Road. They moved from there to a location near the present building, and then to the campus they occupy today, the third location. Some of the early ministers were J. D. Anthony (1847), the Anthony brothers (1865-1869), Reverend Johnson (1869-79), Reverend Cramer (1871), J. W. Stipes (1872), F. F. Reynolds (1873-1874), J. H. Bentley (1875-76), and J. S. Embry (1877-78). Zoar, now a United Methodist Church, is still serving the community today.

On Wednesday, August 19, 1819, Ely Massey, Dicey Parker, Divinity Knight, Sarah Barnett, and Luke Robinson met together and founded Rockbridge Baptist Church. The meeting occurred near the Rock Bridge of the Yellow River, thus the name. The following year a log meeting house was built. It was used until 1825. Another meeting house was built that year. It was used until 1893. In 1893 the church moved two miles north to its current location in Centerville. The original pastor was charter member Luke Robinson. He served 21 years. There is still a church on the Rockbridge Baptist Church site in Centerville. Sadly, Rockbridge Baptist Church is no more.

There's so much history in our little hamlet. I haven't talked about our chapter of the Farmers Alliance. After Reconstruction farming began to recover, even cotton. The problems lay in the high cost of money, transportation, and overwhelming debt. Especially for sharecroppers and small landowners. It was formed in 1888 as a militant agrarian organization to fight these issues, and to give farmers a voice. Our representatives were W. L. Livsey, S. P. Williams, G. M. Brown, and F. J. Livsey. The Farmers Alliance became politically active in 1890 and later became the Populist party.

By 1900 Centerville, and the whole of Gwinnett County was booming. Railroads, trade, and bumper crops all played a part. Still, a soldier or sailor, like Robert L. Norton Sr., coming home to Centerville after WWI saw little change. Cotton was still the king of the crops. The boll weevil was coming but was yet to arrive. It all sounds great, but the boom didn't last. The post-war spike in cotton prices began to sputter, and decline. Slowly at first, then more rapidly. It landed at a nickel a pound. Then came the drought of 1925. It ruined the cotton crop; farming would never be the same after that. Many Centerville men, whose families had farmed the land for several generations, just gave up. They began to look for "public work." The coup-de-grace' was the Great Depression. Hey mister, can you spare a dime? It took a new president and another world war to get us out of the depression.

Centerville remained a sleepy little farming community until the late 60's. Urban sprawl, initially fed by "white flight" from Atlanta, quickly overtook us. Farms became subdivisions, fast food joints, strip-malls, and even a Super Wal-Mart. By the early 80's, Centerville had changed, as all things do with the march of time. Like I said in the first paragraph, that's a brief history. Let's continue and see what else we find.

GRANNY FREEMAN'S TEA CAKE RECIPE

These were always available in Granny Freeman's kitchen. She made a batch two or three times a month. I ate at least one every day when I got home from school. They were love on a plate.

Ingredients

- 4 cups all-purpose flour (you'll also need a little more for rolling)
- 1 teaspoon baking soda
- 2 teaspoons baking powder
- 2 cups sugar
- 2 eggs
- 1/2 cup buttermilk
- 1/2-pound (2 sticks) butter, softened.
- 1 teaspoon vanilla

Instructions

1. Preheat oven to 350 degrees F.
2. In a large bowl sift flour, baking soda, and baking powder together.
3. Add remaining ingredients and blend well. Dough will be soft and wet.
4. On a floured surface shape, the dough into a disk, cover with plastic wrap and refrigerate for 1 hour.
5. Flour surface again and roll dough out until approximately 1/4 inch thick.
6. Cut dough into desired shapes and bake on a slightly greased sheet pan for 10 to 12 minutes.
7. Turn out on a cooling rack and let cool.

Enjoy!

GRANNY FREEMAN

I'll never forget Granny.
Her kindness and gentle spirit molded me
with love unconditional.
Sometimes I hurt her in the folly of my youth,
but she never let on.
Have I followed her example?
I doubt it.
We're cut from different cloth.
I, a rough muslin.
She, the finest silk.
Born before cars and airplanes.
A simpler time.
No electric lights or indoor plumbing.
"Slop jars" at night.
Chickens under the house,
visible through the cracks in the floor.
A thousand stories of the way things used to be.
No, I'll never forget Granny.
I love her.
She's a big part of who I am.
I hope she's proud of me.

CHURCH FLATULENCE

We've all been there.

I was startled. The odor came out of nowhere, rolled over me like fog over the mountains, and vanished just as quickly. I instinctively looked around to see if I could identify the culprit. No one grinned. Flatulence occurred.

It happens all the time. In elevators, trains, hallways, classrooms, and anywhere else people congregate. Oh yes, and cars. Most definitely cars.

Why, you ask? Noise. Anytime you have a crowd of people noise is a naturally occurring phenomenon. It happens at various levels, but even in so called silence it exists. It may be at almost imperceptible levels but it's there. And if there's noise, and there always is, flatulence occurs. That appears to be the rule. But as with every rule there are exceptions. Church comes to mind.

I grew up in the Southern United States. I come from a long line of Methodists. The Methodist church in America has a long tradition of several churches, served by one minister, on what's called a circuit. That goes back to England. The first Methodist circuit rider-preacher in America was Robert Strawbridge. He arrived in 1764 and rode a horse to service the churches on his circuit. He might be in a church every other month. That tradition continues in some places to this day. But I digress.

Zoar Methodist, the little country church I attended, was only a few years off a circuit. That meant that we had services every Sunday and not twice a month. When I was a boy there were a lot of people in church, but very little noise. Unlike today, Church was quiet, a place of reverence. Not a very good place or time for a flatulence occurrence because it could be heard. That was especially true in our church. Our pews were antiques. They were handmade out of wide solid oak boards. Those pews were beautiful, with a kind of rustic elegance that befitted a church founded in 1811. Those pews were also the perfect amplification system for flatulence. One released onto the solid oak of the pew would resonate. Bright, clear tones that could be heard throughout the church. An especially good one could be heard over the pastor's voice. For a teenage boy it was a thing of beauty.

Church back then removed the anonymity of the crowd. It didn't happen often, but when it did it was funny. Laugh out loud, wet your pants funny. At least it was to my best friend, Anthony White, and me. Nothing is funnier than the sound of flatulence. Especially to boys full of the raging hormones of puberty. This presented a problem. Church, by and large, wasn't a place of laughter. Well, maybe the occasional polite giggle at one of the pastor's jokes, but not the uncontrollable belly-laugh.

I remember one time particularly. Waldine Argroves had just delivered a rousing rendition of her signature song, The Holy City. As she took her seat preacher Winn stepped up to the stand and opened his Bible. I still remember his text. It was John 8:12: "Again Jesus spoke to them, saying, "I am the light of the world; he who follows me will not walk in darkness, but will have the light of life." Revised Standard Version of course.

After the prayer he set sail into the sermon. Brother Winn had a deep voice. His delivery was that of an old-time preacher, except no shouting. I loved his preaching. He preached the Word. No holds barred. He came up through the Methodist-Episcopal Church and stayed when they became just Methodists. He couldn't abide the United addition to Methodist. He resigned his credentials and finished his life as a Wesleyan.

Brother Winn was beginning to close when it happened. The violator released what started as a high squeal, just under dog whistle pitch. It quickly dropped several octaves to a low moan, then returned to the squeal for the finish. Total time? 20 plus seconds. And the pew performed flawlessly.

Anthony and I tried not to look at each other. We tried even harder to hold back the full-on belly laugh that was building in us like pressure on a steam boiler. We were shaking so hard trying to stifle the laugh that the pew was rocking. So far so good, but then we heard it. The muffled giggles that began to breakout all over the sanctuary. All was lost. Our laughter exploded from our seat in the back right corner like a broadside from a battleship. Tears flowed freely and we howled. Some adults lost it too.

Preacher Winn, God rest his soul, sensed he was losing control. He rushed through his close and called for *Just as I Am* for the alter call. His wife, Vernice, was also the pianist. The wife as pianist is a long time Methodist tradition that now has crossed denominational lines. Especially in small rural churches. It's sort of a two-for-one deal because the wife is rarely paid. Anyway, Mrs. Winn left off the prelude and jumped right into the first verse.

Anthony and I were dragged out the back door by his mom, Mrs. Evelyn White, before the first chorus. She proceeded to dress us down and even, in true Methodist fashion, questioned whether we'd lost our Salvation. She was just finishing our scolding when Preacher Winn opened the doors. We were truly contrite, and under control, until he winked at us before turning to greet the congregants. We took off running until out of ear shot of Mrs. White, and completely lost it again. To this day I've never laughed that hard. It was painful, but in a good way.

What a day. For years after Anthony and I would break into hysterics at the mention of that Sunday. And Preacher Winn became our all-time favorite pastor. William Maltbie Winn, Jr is the longest serving pastor in Zoar's long history.

TELL HOPPY I'LL BE THERE SOON

One by one their voices fall silent, victims of the passage of time.
Yet their faces still hover in my memory like fog at dawn.
I miss my companions of youth, like my comfortable clothes that were taken in the night by thieves; at least they've disappeared.

Your images remain flickering in a medium of half-tone gray and black.
Theme song refrains harken back to a simpler time, sweet childhood joy.
Granny waiting at the door when I got off the bus with her tea cakes and a glass of cold, cold milk; I can't believe she's gone too?

I rode with you in reruns before I got my lessons, and later in prime time.
Before the days of color tv and rock and roll brought the changes.
Recess at school was filled with talk of you, and many hours were spent pretending I was you in the grassless front yard; only lazy folks had grass.

I've grown older and I haven't seen you in a while: I've spent as much time as I could with you, or at least as much time as adulthood allows.
I am standing at the top of the hill now and you just went

around the curve.

The sound of the hoof beats of your horse echo back from the canyon walls; tell Hoppy I'll be there soon.

JUDY'S FRIED CHICKEN

My wife Judy learned to fry chicken from her Mama, Berry Lee Smith Harrison. Mrs. Berry Lee was a master, and Judy learned her lessons well. I would say its finger licking good, but I can't afford a lawsuit.

Ingredients

- 1 (3- to 4-pound) whole chicken, cut into pieces*
- 1 teaspoon salt
- 1 teaspoon pepper
- 2 cups buttermilk
- Self-rising flour
- Vegetable oil

*Note: you can use your favorite pieces of chicken, you don't have to use the whole bird. I like the breast. Judy prefers the thighs and or legs. What's your favorite?

Instructions

1. Sprinkle chicken with salt and pepper. Place chicken in a shallow dish or zip-top plastic bag and add buttermilk. Cover or seal, and chill at least 2 hours.
2. Remove chicken from buttermilk, discarding buttermilk. Dredge chicken in flour.
3. Pour the vegetable oil to a depth of 1 1/2 inches in a deep skillet, preferably one made of cast iron. Heat the oil. Judy's Mama never used a thermometer. Today we'll use one to ensure the oil is at 360°, the perfect temperature for frying chicken. Add the chicken slowly, a few pieces at a time; cover and cook 6 minutes. Uncover chicken and cook 9 minutes. Turn chicken; cover and cook 6 minutes. Uncover and cook 5 to 9 minutes, turning chicken the last 3 minutes for even browning, if necessary. Drain on paper towels. Serve hot.

Enjoy with any or all the following sides: sliced fresh tomatoes, creamed corn, butterbeans, green beans, or mashed potatoes. Don't forget the homemade biscuits. Lord have mercy!

I GREW UP IN THE EASTERN SHADOWS OF STONE MOUNTAIN

For the first 13 years of my life Stone Mountain Park didn't exist. The Stone Mountain Memorial Association created it. The lake, and all the other stuff was built between 1958 and 1965. The park officially opened on April 14, 1965. Do you see the irony, or creepiness? That's 100 years to the day after Lincoln's assassination. Anyway, back then US 78 ran right beneath the carving. A big pile of rock and other debris lay at the base of the mountain under the unfinished sculpture.

The "gray whale" bubbled up some 300-350 million years ago according to geologists. It's what they call a monadnock. It formed underground during the creation of the Blue Ridge and Southern Appalachian Mountains. Magma swelled from the Earth's core and solidified into granite. It cooled five to ten miles below the surface. Erosion took care of the rest. The mountain's top is 1,686 feet above sea level and 825 feet above the surrounding woods. There are clear freshwater pools on the summit. These pools contain clam shrimp and fairy shrimp. Wildflowers abound too. Along the trails you can see more than 120 different kinds. Most are native to the Southern Appalachians. Some are rare and protected.

Archeology in the Stone Mountain area shows human activity at the big rock going back 9,000 years. Europeans first heard of the mountain in the 1540's. The Spaniard DeSoto was told of an inland mountain. The natives said it was "very high, shining when the sun set like a fire." In the late seventeenth century English traders saw Stone Mountain for the first time. When they climbed to the top, they found it encircled by a stacked rock wall. The wall was like the one found on Georgia's Fort Mountain today. Inside the wall they found what later was called the Devil's Crossroads. Devil's Crossroads was a flat boulder roughly 200 feet across and 5 to 10 feet thick. It was split by two straight cracks about four feet wide. One ran north-south and the other ran east-west. The cracks joined at right angles in the center of the boulder. The "crossroads" was capped by another flat rock 20 feet in diameter.

In response to the increasing threat of European intrusion, surviving tribes formed alliances during the late 18th century. These became known as the Creek Confederation. Stone Mountain lay between the Creek Confederation and the Cherokee nation. The mountain that had always been sacred now became an important meeting place. Two major trails, the Hightower, and the Standing Peachtree connected it to the eastern part of the state. Still, European settlers increasingly moved into the area. In the early 19th century, the area was known as Rock Mountain, and then New Gibraltar for a while. After the founding of DeKalb County in 1822 the name became Stone Mountain. It was a natural recreation area. Young couples on dates road there on horseback and climbed to the top. The mountain was, and still is, easy to climb.

Entrepreneur Aaron Cloud built a 165 feet wooden observation tower on the mountain in 1838. It was destroyed by a storm and replaced by a much smaller one in 1851. By then visitors could travel by train. Cloud by this time also had a restaurant and club on top.

Granite quarrying started in the 1830s. It became a major industry on the completion of a railroad spur to the quarry in 1847. This spur line was rebuilt by the Georgia Railroad Company in 1869. Stone Mountain granite became prized for building. It was used all over the world. You'll find it in the locks of the Panama Canal, the steps to the East Wing of the US Capital and the Imperial Hotel in Tokyo. Quarrying during earlier periods also destroyed several spectacular geological features on Stone Mountain. The Devil's Crossroads formation was the first to go. It contained some of the finest granite there.

In 1887, Stone Mountain was purchased for $45,000 by the Venable Brothers, Sam, and William. They quarried granite there for 24 years. At their deaths the mountain passed to their descendants. It was purchased by the State of Georgia in 1958 "as a memorial to the Confederacy." But friends, it got interesting way before that.

Let's back up a little bit...how'd this whole carving thing get started? The written evidence points to Francis Ticknor, a nineteenth century doctor and poet. Doctor Ticknor hailed from Jones County, Georgia. His 1869 poem, "Stone Mountain," proposed a monument to Alexander Hamilton Stephens. Stephens, a Georgian, was the former vice-president of the Confederacy. William H. Terrell, an Atlanta attorney and son of a Confederate veteran, suggested a permanent memorial publicly on May 26, 1914, in an editorial for the *Atlanta Constitution*. Three weeks later, Georgian John Temple Graves, editor of the *New York American*, suggested a 70-foot statue of Robert E. Lee. The idea was beginning to get legs.

C. Helen Plane was a charter member of the United Daughters of the Confederacy. She was also the Honorary Life President of the Georgia UDC. She made herself the driving force for the project. Mrs. Plane sought and got the approval of the Georgia UDC to set up the UDC Stone Mountain Memorial Association. She chose the sculptor Gutzon Borglum for the project and invited him to visit the mountain. It's said she wouldn't shake his hand. Although he was a member of the Ku Klux Klan he was, after all, a Yankee. She met him at the Atlanta train station. She then took him to her family's summer home, Mont Rest, at the foot of the mountain. It was there she introduced him to Sam Venable, an active Klan member and owner of the mountain. More about that later.

Borglum's original plan was, shall we say, ambitious. It called for 5 groups of figures. There'd be 65 mounted officers representing the states (to be chosen by the states). General Nathan Bedford Forrest and his cavalry. A total of 700 to 1,000 figures, each from 35 feet to 50 feet high. In addition, he planned to cut a room 60 feet into the mountain. The room was to be 320 feet wide, and 40 feet high, and faced by 13 columns. Nothing this grandiose had ever been conceived, much less attempted, but there's more. Mrs. Plane, ever the Klan supporter, suggested an addition to the design in a letter to Borglum:

"I feel that it is due to the Ku Klux Klan which saved us from Negro domination and carpet-bag rule, that it be immortalized on Stone Mountain. Why not represent a small group of them in their nightly uniform approaching in the distance?"

Wow! Just Wow!

Venable deeded the north face of the mountain to the UDC in 1916. There was only one condition: Complete the monument in 12 years.

Financial and technical problems plagued the project from the get-go. Various fundraisers were attempted by the UDC. None more ambitious than the Confederate 50 cent piece. Yes, the issue of a commemorative 50 cent coin. After much arm twisting the U.S. Mint issued a 1925 Commemorative silver "Stone Mountain" half dollar. This required the approval of the 1926 Congress and President Calvin Coolidge. These coins had

Robert E. Lee and Stonewall Jackson on the front. The back
has an eagle with wings stretched. It represents liberty and
is perched on a mountaintop. There are 35 stars in the field.
They're supposed to represent the number of states at the start
of the Civil War. Wrong! There were in fact 34 in 1861. To this
day it's still one of the largest commemorative coin issues in
U.S. history. As fundraisers go, this was a flop, as were most of
the other things they tried.

Conflicts between Borglum and the SMMA led to his firing in
1925. Some say it was because he took 7 months to design
the coin. Others say it was his arrogance. Either way, He
destroyed his models claiming they were his property. The
Association disagreed and had a warrant issued for his arrest.
Warned about the warrant Borglum escaped to North Carolina.
The kerfuffle was highly publicized. During this time there
was also discord between Sam Venable, the Association, and
Association president Hollins Randolph.

Borglum's partially completed face of Lee was blasted off the
mountain. This was ordered by Henry Augustus Lukeman,
the newly hired sculptor. He started work on his design in
1925. Lukeman's carving included the 3 central figures of the
Confederacy, Lee, Jackson, and Davis, on horseback. He set to
work with pneumatic drills. By 1928 (the original deadline)
only Lee's new head was complete. The SMMA was out of
money. As agreed, the Venable family took back their property.
The carving would remain untouched for 36 years.

The Ku Klux Klan and Stone Mountain are forever linked.
Sociologist James W. Loewen said that the mountain was, "the
most sacred site to members of the second and third national
klans." Most scholars agree on the rebirth of the second Klan. It
was as inspired by the January 1915 release of Klan-glorifying
film, *The Birth of a Nation*. That silent film premiered in
Riverside, California. In August 1915 a Jewish businessman,
Leo Frank, from Atlanta was lynched for the supposed murder

of Mary Phagan. The stage was set. On November 25, 1915, Thanksgiving Day, 15 robed and hooded "charter members" of the new Klan, met at the summit of Stone Mountain. Their purpose? To create a new iteration of the Klan. They were led by William J. Simmons, a Methodist minister. The group also included two elderly members of the original Klan. Their ceremony included an altar covered with a flag. Upon the altar lay an open Bible. Their new twist was the burning of a 16-foot cross. The first Klan didn't burn crosses.

One of the fifteen that November night was James R. Venable. James was the nephew of Sam Venable. He stood next to his uncle Sam as the cross was lit. James became a prominent lawyer in Atlanta. Later, he was instrumental in the founding of one of the factions of the 3rd Klan. Advancing to the position of Imperial Wizard of the National Knights of the Ku Klux Klan. James owned land at the base of the mountain he'd inherited from his ancestors. In October of 1923 he granted the Klan an easement. The easement gave them the perpetual right to hold celebrations anytime they wanted. The property was condemned in 1960 at the request of the Stone Mountain Memorial Association, but that didn't stop them.

The Klan held cross-burnings at the summit of the mountain from 1915 onward. This practice finally came to an end in 1962. The Klan wanted to hold a cross-burning to protest the NAACP national convention in Atlanta. The SMMA didn't want either group using state property for demonstrations. They convinced Governor Ernest Vandiver to have state troopers stop the Klan proceedings. 70 troopers tried to do so. Several hundred Klansmen were gathered at the base of the mountain, and violence ensued. The Klansmen were armed with nightsticks, flashlights, and rocks. Outnumbered, the troopers negotiated a truce with the local Klan Grand Dragon. The Klansmen agreed to stop the violence. If, 20 of their number were allowed to climb the mountain for a "religious ceremony." This they did, and instead of burning a cross they lit a flare.

Back to the carving...In 1960 the Stone Mountain Confederate Memorial Advisory Committee was formed. It was made up of 6 internationally known figures in the art world. A competition was held, and 9 world-renowned sculptors submitted designs for a new sculpture.

In 1963 the Stone Mountain Memorial Association chose Walker Kirkland Hancock to complete the carving. Work resumed in 1964. A new technique utilizing thermo-jet torches was used to carve the granite. The chief carver was Roy Faulkner. Faulkner was a marine veteran with a talent for using the thermo-jet torch. He could remove tons of stone in a day. For over 8 years people could see and hear the workmen and their jet torches.

The figures were completed with the detail of a fine painting. Eyebrows, fingers, buckles, and even strands of hair were fine carved with a small thermo-jet torch.

Hancock's design was a scaled down version of Lukeman's. The finished work is much larger than it appears. The carved surface measures three-acres. That's larger than a football field and Borglum's Mount Rushmore. The carving of the 3 men towers 400 feet above the ground. It measures 90 by 190 feet and is recessed 42 feet into the mountain. The deepest point of the carving is at Lee's elbow, which is 12 feet to the mountain's surface. Workers could easily stand on a horse's ear or inside a horse's mouth to escape a rain shower. A dedication ceremony for the Confederate Memorial Carving was held on May 9, 1970. Finishing touches were completed in 1972. It remains the largest bas-relief sculpture in the world.

Controversy still swirls around the carving. Some are for keeping it right where it is. Others have already ordered sandblasters to take it off. As Sam Nunn, the former senator from Georgia, used to say, "Some of my friends are for it. Some of my friends are against it. I'm for my friends." Seriously, I hope we can reach a compromise. The whole truth needs to be told. Right now, all we have is a shrine to the bull feathers that is the Lost Cause.

I'll never forget rounding the curve on that old 2-lane highway, crossing the creek, and seeing the mountain. On Christmas day, 1961, it looked like a big ball, half buried, and covered in ice. Ice was everywhere. The boughs of the trees were all bent over too. It was picture post card stuff, a real winter wonderland for sure. Thank God the roads weren't slick. We made it to Daddy Bob and Nanny Pat's just fine. Another great Christmas. It wasn't snow, but it was enough to thrill a southern boy's heart.

If you want to know more about Stone Mountain here's two books I highly recommend:

Carved in Stone, The History of Stone Mountain by David B. Freeman (no relation)

The Man Who Carved Stone Mountain (about Roy Faulkner, the man who finished the carving) by Donna Faulkner Barron and Kay Jones Stowe

KING COTTON COMES DOWN

I stood in the edge of a cotton field
just after the sun went down.
The puffy white bolls seemed to glow,
as the moon rose orange and round.

The sight gave rise to somber thoughts
of a time not so long ago.
When cotton was the major crop,
and most ground looked white like snow.

The various soils of my Georgia home
was perfect for the "Lamb Tree."
Here cotton grew fast, tall, and healthy.
Profits soared, especially along the sea.

When cotton was King in the "peach" state
it was shipped all over the world.
This ancient, poet praised, fiber
was precious wherever flags unfurled.

An economy built upon the backs of men,
folks as dark as the midnight sky.
Their hands were perfect for its picking.
Without them the trade would die.

From its earliest days this country of ours
was built on the backs of slaves.
The money they earned made many rich,

but they went destitute to their graves.

It would take a war to overthrow this king.
Horrible bloodshed would set his captives free.
Penance came for the planters afterwards.
Their lives a shadow of what they used to be.

In 1892 a bug crossed the Rio Grande,
and slowly crawled north and east.
By the 1920's cotton lost its crown,
succumbing to the weevil "beast".

Cotton still grows on these red clay hills,
but no longer in the quantities of old.
It was dark when I made my way back to the truck,
and the night had turned windy and cold.

MOM'S OLD FASHIONED COCONUT CAKE

(Recipe is over 100 years old)

Daddy loved this cake. In fact, everyone that's ever had a piece love it. Unless they don't like coconut. Their loss, and more for us, right? Seriously, this is the most moist cake you'll ever put in your mouth.

Layers

- 1 teaspoon vanilla
- 1 cup shortening (Crisco)
- 2 cups sugar
- 1 teaspoon (heaping) baking powder
- 4 eggs
- 3 ½ cups sifted flour (cake or plain)

- 1 cup milk

Instructions

1. Mix all the above and divide into 3, 9-inch cake pans (lightly greased).
2. Bake at 350 degrees for approximately 30 minutes.

Icing

- 3 cups milk
- 1-stick butter
- 3 cups sugar
- 1 large, or 2 small bags of frozen coconut

Instructions

1. Boil all the above ingredients until the sugar is completely melted.
2. Punch holes in layers and pour icing over them as you stack them.

SOUTHERN, IT'S WHAT I AM

I've always spoken with a Southern drawl. It's all I heard during my formative years. I'm proud of the language which I speak. It's music to my ears. Uneducated folks poke fun at our Southern accent. Maybe that's why it ain't used much anymore. What bugs me is most people don't know it's an old language. The Elizabethan English brought to this country's Southern parts by the Scotch-Irish and English. Also, contributions snuck in from Huguenots, Quakers, and Germans.

Our Southern mountains are the last bastions of this dialect. In many places in the South it's gone, or as the late Zell Miller said, "Purt Nigh Gone." It started dying out as our young people grew up and went away to school, or to the big cities seeking work. Then new families came. They settled on land where we'd had the same neighbors for years. But the old tongue still lives. The one used 250 years ago when the Scotch-Irish began settling the mountains. The Scotch-Irish were driven from Northern Ireland by the Stuart Kings. They first landed in Maryland and Virginia. They migrated as far west as the Indians and French allowed, then moved southward to the rugged mountains and fertile valleys we know as Appalachia. These hardy Presbyterians were accompanied by Virginia English, Huguenots, Pennsylvania Quakers, Polatine Germans and various other dissatisfied Protestant sects.

They sought isolation from the world. Their language, tools, and knowledge were isolated with them. Suspended in time they relied on their skills and their culture. For years the only changes they knew were those of birth and death. They were independent and rugged individuals. Honest and shrewd they worked hard on the ridges and valleys to support their families. They were, and still are, proud people.

If you arrived at their humble cabin here's what you might hear; "We's po folks and hit ain't much but you are welcome to what they is." If Shakespeare were there, he would've felt right at home. Maybe painful and ungrammatical to modern ears, it would have been very familiar to the Bard. Southern speech is a spoken rather than a written language. You need to hear it to appreciate it. The use of double nouns is common. Words like hosepipe, biscuit-bread, church-house, widow-woman, preacher-man, rifle-gun, pork-meat. Examples of Chaucerian English; beasties, nesties, costes, postes, the plural of nouns and verbs with "es" and "ies" instead of "s." Another well-known custom is using a final "n" instead of "s". As in; his'n, our'n, your'n, her'n, instead of his, ours, yours, hers.

The uses of Elizabethan terms were very common. I heard these terms every day as I was growing up, and still do occasionally. "afeared" instead of afraid, "stove" instead of jabbed, "ashamed" instead of bashful, "drap" instead of drop, "spell" instead of time or while, "fix" instead of prepare, "reckon" instead of think, "aim" instead of intend, "kiver" instead of cover, "nigh" instead of near, "betwist" instead of between, "heap" instead of many, "puny" instead of sickly, "plunder" instead of possessions, "misery" instead of pain, "ingern's" instead of onions. Remember how Shakespeare had Othello say, "I aim to."

I love the Southern dialect because I grew up with it and when I occasionally hear it it's like coming home. I seldom speak it myself and as the old ones pass away it may be disappearing forever. I hope not, but I'm afeared it is.

Most of this knowledge was gained by reading the great Southern apologist and educator Dr. Cleanth Brooks. Dr. Brooks is my muse.

I WAIT

I wait.
In waiting I'll find peace.
Peace that brings release.
I struggle as I wait, but
I wait.

I wait.
Though often I don't see.
Seeing won't set me free.
I must struggle deep inside so
I wait.

I wait.
My strength is waning,
Yet I must continue.
I struggle and I rest and
I wait.

I wait.
I wait.
I wait.

GRANNY FREEMAN'S CHESS PIE WITH STEWED DRIED APPLES

Ingredients

- 1 unbaked pie crust, store bought or homemade
- 1/2 cup butter, melted and cooled
- 4 large eggs
- 1 1/2 cup granulated sugar
- 2 tablespoons cornmeal
- 1 tablespoon all-purpose flour
- 1/4 teaspoon salt
- 1/4 cup 2 % milk, room temperature
- 1 tablespoon white vinegar
- 1 1/2 teaspoons vanilla extract
- 2 cups dried apples

Instructions

1. Preheat the oven to 350 degrees Fahrenheit.
2. Make a homemade pie crust (like Granny) or use a store-bought pie crust. Roll it out and place it into a pie dish. Finish the edges however you like!
3. Melt the butter in saucepan or microwave then allow to cool.

4. In a small mixing bowl whisk the eggs until blended well, set aside.
5. In a large mixing bowl add the granulated sugar, cornmeal, flour, and salt. Stir until combined.
6. Add the milk, vinegar, vanilla, and whisked eggs to the bowl of dry ingredients. Whisk together until incorporated.
7. Mix in the cooled butter until smooth and combined.
8. Stew the dried apples, allow to cool, and spread evenly over bottom of pie crust.
9. Pour the batter into the prepared crust. Carefully place the pie on a baking sheet and into the preheated oven.
10. Bake at 350° F for 45 minutes to 1 hour or the until edges are set. It's normal for the center to wiggle slightly. Cover the pie with foil for the last 10 minutes if the edges of the crust are getting too brown.
11. Allow the pie to cool for 1 hour before slicing and serving.

Cover and store leftover pie (Yeah, Right!) in the refrigerator.

RECONNECTION

Riding through the heartland along Georgia's eastern back roads.

The corn is so green it looks black, and the dirt is gray.

The black and white Holsteins look as though they've been scattered across the bright green hillocks by the hand of God.

The silos point like stubby fingers toward the sky on the Mennonite farms.

Their simple churches and simpler faith knit the fabric of land and flesh together.

I notice a doe standing in the edge of a cotton field.

Timidly waiting for me to pass.

The bright, reddish color of her coat against the dark brown-green pine forest is beautiful.

Off in the distance an anvil-head rises toward Heaven preparing to bless the hot afternoon with its gift.

It is a pastoral scene; Peace defined in nature's majesty.

I sigh a contented sigh.

I feel connected to myself and my roots again.

That which was thought to be lost was rediscovered in the beauty of an early summer, Georgia afternoon.

MY DOG REB

In the mid 1960's a very religious dog came into my life. Our friends, Earl and Waldine Argroves collie had a litter of puppies. I wanted one. Being a big fan of the TV show "Lassie" that made perfect sense. At least it did to a teenage boy. Mrs. Argroves heard I wanted a puppy. Guess what? She gave me one. I named him Reb. Reb was the first dog in the family not named Skip.

Now about Reb's religion. On July 1, 1970, Dr. Nat Long followed Brother Winn as Pastor at Zoar. Dr. Long was a graduate of the Yale School of Divinity. Though he was highly educated, he was a down-to-earth guy. In my experience that's not always the case. Anyway, Dr. Long, was impressed by my church-going-dog. He noticed that Reb kept regular attendance at meetings. Once he learned Reb's name the 2 became fast friends.

Dr. Long, and his wife Olive had a regular Sunday routine. They arrived at Zoar a few minutes before 10. Sunday School started at 10. Mrs. Long went into the church. She started the chimes and prepared the music. Yes, she was also the church pianist. Starting the chimes consisted of turning on the record player and starting the record. The scratchy music was blasted across Centerville via the lone loudspeaker in the steeple. All very high-tech for 1970. The chimes were a gift to Zoar from Brother Winn. While his wife was busy in the church Dr. Long sat in the car doing some last-minute sermon preparation. Soon after the chimes started Reb would trot toward the church. Upon arrival he'd cross the lawn and head to the Long's car. He'd patiently wait for Dr. Long to open the door. You see, Reb always got a pat the head, and a kind word. After their little ritual, he would go and lie down on the lawn in front of the church, Reb, not Dr. Long.

Reb attended Sunday School, Church, Youth Meetings, Funerals, Weddings, Homecoming Dinners, Choir Practices, Vacation Bible School, and Revivals.

One Sunday morning, before Sunday School, Dr. Long and Reb were going through their routine. He was patting Reb on the head and bragging on him to Mrs. Argroves. He said, "The Freemans have trained Reb well. I believe that a dog that goes to church so religiously ought to go to heaven." Mrs. Argroves replied, "Well, I want you to remember that Reb was an Argroves before he was a Freeman! We gave him to Terry as a puppy." About that time, Mrs. Laura Johnson was passing by. Mrs. Johnson is a precious lady. There's no nonsense in her, and she's a woman of few words. Dr. Long said to her, "Laura, you're a lady of good judgment! Don't you think that Reb ought to go to heaven?" She just kept walking. As she did, she shouted back, "Of course! I thought that was a foregone conclusion!" Well, everyone who knew Reb thought he ought to go to heaven.

On Sunday December 10, 1972, Dr. Long was preoccupied and didn't notice that Reb wasn't there for Sunday School. About 3 minutes to 11 o'clock my cousin Kathy Attaway, came up on the platform and whispered in his ear, "Reb was hit by a car and killed!" During the announcements, with tears in his eyes, he told the church of Reb's passing. Everyone knew Reb. Some other folks cried too. You could feel the sadness in the room.

I know I'll see Reb and Dr. Long again. The Winns, Olive, and Waldine too, and all the other saints that have gone before.

THIS IS A CEMETERY

This is a Cemetery...
Lives are commemorated.
Deaths are recorded.
Families are reunited.
Memories are tangible, and love is undisguised.

This is a Cemetery...
Communities accord respect.
Families bestow honor.
Historians seek information.
Our ancestral heritage is thereby enriched.

This is a Cemetery...
Tribute is paid.
Accomplishments are celebrated.
It's a place where
testimonies of love, devotion and pride are carved in stone.

This is a Cemetery...
A place of perpetual record.
A source of comfort to the living.
A history of a people.
A record of yesterday and a sanctuary of peace and quiet today.

This is a Cemetery...

THE TOMATO INCIDENT

Having a vegetable garden in the South is akin to breathing. Every true Southerner has or has had one. Even if it's only a patio tomato in a pot on the balcony of their apartment. Each region has vegetable prejudice, or should I say preference? Some love yellow squash. Recently the alien zucchini has gained popularity. Who ever heard of a green squash? Some folks plant cucumbers. What does burpless mean, and how does that work? Everyone has a personal favorite variety of green bean. The Good Lord only knows how many different beans and peas there are. However, there's one thing we all agree on…tomatoes.

Did you know the humble tomato was once feared in Europe? For over 600 years they believed that witches used them to cast spells. By the early 1700's witch fear was dying out. Soon someone tasted one, and they became popular. So popular that only the rich could afford them. By the late 1700's the fear returned. Europeans came to believe they were poisonous. Why'd they believe this obvious untruth? Remember only the rich ate them. European aristocrats ate their tomatoes off pewter plates. Pewter has a high lead content. The rich folks died from lead poisoning.

My parents worked in Atlanta. That left me, Papa, and Granny to plant and tend to the garden. We got our tomato plants at Brannan's store. They came bare rooted in bundles of 50, wrapped in newspaper and held together by a rubber band. Mr.

Brannan kept the plants in a number 2 washtub. He put just enough water in the tub to cover the roots. He carried Big Boy and Rutgers. We only planted Rutgers. The Rutgers variety was developed at Rutgers University in 1934. At one time it was the most popular tomato in the world. We like its combination of acidity and sweetness. It makes a great tomato sammich.

Papa and I handled the planting. Granny's job came when it was time to can some for winter. This usually meant between 50 and 75 Mason jars of deliciousness. By his side I learned how to plant a garden. Papa laid off the rows with our mule, George. We'd put all the seed vegetables in first. The tomatoes were planted last. Here's how we put them out. Papa took the hoe and dug holes in the row about eighteen inches apart. My job was to come behind him and fill the holes with water. I carried a 2-gallon galvanized bucket and the dipper we used at the well. Then we'd both stick them in the ground. The plants were almost buried. We left about 2 inches showing. More water was applied after the burial. I also learned what happened if I accidentally stepped on a plant. Papa said a word I thought meant something that beavers built. Plant, hoe, sweat, and repeat the last 2. It was dirty work. Especially for a young boy. But I loved those tomatoes. They were well worth the effort.

Harvest time went something like this.

"Papa, I'm hot."

"Me too. Quit whining."

Two-minute pause, and then.

"Papa, I'm tired."

"Me too. Keep picking."

"Papa, I'm thirsty."

The last whine drew a colorful word. This was accompanied by Papa's wrinkled forehead, and squinty stare. I grew silent.

In the silence a plan began to form in my ten-year-old brain. Tomatoes were for eating, but that wasn't all. Papa had his back to me. The peck basket by his side on the ground. He was bent over carefully selecting tomatoes for Granny to can. He shifted slightly to allow the hot afternoon breeze to pass between the bib of his overalls and his sweaty t-shirt. The butt of his Red Camel "overhauls", as he called them, made a very tempting target. I was sorely tempted, and soon yielded there unto. Grabbing a small tomato with a tiny rabbit nibble I reared back and let'er fly. Papa kept picking. The tomato sailed wide. He didn't even know I threw it. Time to kick my game up a notch.

"Heads up!" I yelled as I let flung another juicy red orb. Hearing my shout, Papa stood and turned in time to receive the tomato right between the eyes. Pulp, seed, and juice trickled down his face. It dripped off his nose and covered the front his overalls. I knew I was dead. I could almost feel his large, callused hand clamping down on an ear. In my imagination I saw him marching me to the house. When we got near the shrubbery he said, "Pick me a good switch." Papa's switch of choice was a yellow bell limb. They're long and firm, with just the right amount of flex. I saw myself breaking one off the bush. I handed it to him. He administered justice swiftly and mercilessly. I could almost feel my bare legs stinging.

"You little turd," he sputtered as he wiped tomato off his face. Then, to my amazement, he grinned. This scared me. What did that grin mean? It didn't take long to find out. He stooped down, grabbed a tomato, and fired it right back at me. "You missed!" I taunted. "You throw like an old man." "Old man?", he yelled, "I'll show you how an old man throws." He grabbed the biggest tomato he could find and hurled it my way. I tried to turn away but wasn't quick enough. It struck me with a thump and squish in my right ear. Game on.

Younger and faster, I fired three tomatoes to his one. I threw, he hollered; he threw, I whooped. Soon we were flinging Rutgers as fast as we could. Laughter exploded with each toss. It was all fun until his last magnificent throw.

It was a beauty. It must have traveled at least 40 feet. He threw it like a fastball. I felt the whoosh as it sailed over my head. Then his expression changed. He stopped throwing. I turned to look behind me. Fluttering on the clothesline was, a large, formerly pure white sheet. Granny washed early that morning, and I'm sure it was almost dry. The sheet now had a red starburst pattern that seemed to get bigger with each slimy drip. Before I could even turn back, I heard the snarl, "Look at what you made me do! Get your little butt over here right now." Getting my little behind anywhere near Papa was the farthest thing from my mind. I nervously called out, "Got to go, I hear Granny calling me."

"You little buzzard, you know your Granny ain't calling you. Get over here." By this time Papa was talking to my back. I was over the garden fence and charging across the neighbor's field. I was making a beeline for Zoar Church Road. I'd seen that wrath-of-God look on his face. Even at that tender age I knew you didn't mess with God. It turned out that "God" could do more than look vengeful. Papa scrambled over that fence and came after me. Aunt Lucy, Papa, and Granny's second child, and her husband Sam Brodnax lived next door. I meet the school bus at their house, so I knew the lay of the land. My plan was to take refuge in one of their outbuildings. I looked over my shoulder. To my shock he was gaining on me. This called for a change of plan. I hit the road near Aunt Lucy's driveway and turned left toward home. I started walking faster. So did he. I broke into a slow trot. On he came. Seeing the hill in front of the house ahead, I decided to charge up it as fast as I could. Surely this would leave him behind. Cresting the hill and out of breath, I paused, hands on knees, breathing hard.

"Wait, hold on." Looking up, I saw Papa, wheezing and

wobbling, coming up that hill. He wasn't moving quickly, but he was moving.

"OK, OK, I'll wait," I panted. I was tired. I was also convinced my life would end right there, in the middle of the road. Might as well get it over with.

Trudging up to me, Papa was a mess. His hat was soaked. He smelled of sweat and tomatoes. His clothes were sweaty and showed tears from the fence climbing. At best, I expected a furious tongue lashing, but I feared the worst. As he came up, I braced myself. The last thing I expected was the tomato he slipped from his pocket. He proceeded to shove the tomato down the front of my shirt. Grinning, he wrapped me in a fierce bear hug, smashing the tomato. He whispered in my ear, "That's the most fun I've had in years. Thanks, Bud." We walked toward the house hand in hand. Granny stood on the porch, hands on hips, with a puzzled look on her face. I was sure she hadn't been to the clothesline.

What a great day. Every time I eat a tomato sandwich the afore described incident comes flooding back into my mind. I never complained about working in the garden again. I sure do miss you, Papa.

THOUGHTS ON AGING

When I was young
My life was carefree.
I think I was me.
When I was young.

When I was young
And running fast
I thought it would last.
When I was young.

When I was young
And love was around
I thought it'd been found.
When I was young.

When I was young
And saw death
It took my breath.
When I was young.

When I was Young
And people weren't real
I knew what to feel.
When I was young.

Now that I'm old
I ask, "Where did time go"?
I won't ever know

Now that I am old.

Now that I'm old
And life slips away,
I have much left to say
Now that I am old.

CHRISTMAS, 1959

Christmas was always a magical time at our house. I was triple blessed. I lived with my parents, Morris, and Molly Freeman. My paternal grandparents, Nathaniel, and Maude Freeman, lived with us too. My maternal grandfather and step-grandmother, Robert and Pat Attaway, lived a few miles away in Stone Mountain. I was smothered with much love every day. On Christmas day presents covered me like a tidal wave. Yes, I was triple blessed.

The weather Christmas day 1959 was cool, but not cold. Our family tradition was to have Christmas at home with Papa and Granny. We had my Santa Claus time, opened the other presents, and had a huge country breakfast. I can still smell the hot biscuits, country ham, eggs, and coffee. There were also plenty of homemade preserves that Granny put up over the summer. About 1:30 or 2:00 we headed to Stone Mountain. At Daddy Bob and Nanny Pat's, we'd do it all over again. Yes Sir, high times for a 7-year-old.

I slept in the den at the homeplace. It was the center of our family's social activity, and my bedroom. Later, our black and white TV would land there too. I got to watch "Daniel Boone" while lying in my bed. Anyway, I remember waking up early that Christmas and looking out the window to see if there was snow. A Southern boys dream; snow for Christmas! Alas, there was none, so I quickly ran to the living room to see what Santa Claus had brought.

Papa and Granny were in the kitchen with Mom and Dad when I went flying by the door. They were having a cup of coffee. Granny had mine fixed; 2/3 coffee 1/3 milk and 2 teaspoons of sugar. I ignored that. I was after the presents. When I burst through the arched doorway to the living room my heart almost stopped. There it was the red Huffy bicycle that I wanted. It even had the battery-powered light on the front fender. I also got a Roy Rogers set complete with gun, holster, hat, and guitar. I didn't know where to begin. I was overwhelmed by the bounty, and the joy of it all.

My Dad took the photo at the beginning of this chapter after I'd settled down. Papa and the guitar were a hoot, but I love the look on his face. He is Grand Ole Opry ready. Granny got a kick out of it too, as you can see. After the photo-op was concluded we tore into the rest of the presents. Laughter filled the room and jokes and wrapping paper flew. Christmas 1959 was a special year at our house. One of many we've had over the years. My Mom was the custodian of the magic. She left us July 21, 2021. She loved Christmas.

Immerse yourself in the joy that is Christmas. In your busyness don't forget that Babe in the Manager. After all, it's His birthday celebration. As you prepare for the joy of this Christmas carve out some time for your family too. Family is important especially in times like these. Now, with Tiny Tim I say, "And may God Bless us everyone."

NANNY PAT'S MINCEMEAT PIE

This pie was my special Christmas treat. Nanny Pat made it just for me. No, really. I was the only one in the family who ate it. Everyone else thought it was horrible. Thus, more for me, and believe you me I could eat it all. Is there any wonder I wore husky pants when I was a boy?

Ingredients

- 1 jar (20.5 oz) ready-to-use mincemeat (2 cups)
- 1 ½ cups chopped pecans
- 1 Gala apple, peeled, chopped (1 1/2 cups)
- ½ cup chopped dried Calimyrna figs
- 1/3 cup packed brown sugar
- 1/3 cup brandy
- 2 teaspoons grated lemon peel
- 1 box (14.1 oz) premade pie crusts (2 Count), softened as directed on box

Instructions

1. In medium bowl, stir together mincemeat, pecans,

apple, figs, brown sugar, brandy, and lemon peel. Cover; refrigerate at least 8 hours.

2. Remove pie filling from refrigerator and stand at room temperature 30 minutes.
3. Meanwhile, heat oven to 425°F.
4. Make pie crusts as directed on box for Two-Crust Pie using 9-inch pie plate.
5. Stir filling well; pour into crust-lined plate.
6. Top with second crust and flute; cut slits in several places.
7. Bake on lowest oven rack 40 to 45 minutes or until pastry is golden brown.
8. Cool completely on cooling rack, about 5 hours.

IF THAT'S COUNTRY I'LL...WELL, YOU KNOW

My dad had a 1957 Chevrolet pickup. He and I spent many hours running errands or just riding around in that old truck. The radio stayed on WPLO 590 on the AM dial. There was no FM dial. WPLO was the powerhouse country station in Atlanta. James Clemens, one of their top jocks, was the first to play the Freddie Hart song *Easy Loving*. It was a B-side, but Clemens thought it was better than the A-side. *Easy Loving* became Hart's first Number 1 on the country charts. Anyway, I became a big fan of Merle Haggard in that old truck. I heard my first Porter Waggoner / Dolly Parton duet sitting next to Dad. Although I strayed into rock-and-roll for a while, country stayed in my heart. Thanks Dad.

Well, up in Nashville the Gaylord Corporation and WSM have a building. It is a lovely place: a very impressive concert hall. In fact, I'd be willing to call it grand, but it ain't the Opry. Sorry if this offends you. Just hang on I ain't through yet.

First, a little history. The Grand Ole Opry was originally known as the WSM Barn Dance. Its first broadcast was made from that station's small fifth floor Studio A on November 28, 1925. WSM was and is owned by the National Life and Accident Insurance Company. WSM started as a community service and marketing tool by the insurer. They hoped they could pioneer a new way to sell insurance. It's call letters WSM are short for the company motto "We Shield Millions." "Uncle" Jimmy Thompson, who claimed he could "fiddle the bugs off tater a vine," was the lead performer. The cast included Dr. Humphrey Bate and his daughter Alcyone, the Crook Brothers, and Kirk McGee.

The show eventually moved to Studio B of WSM. Another room in the National Life and Accident Insurance Building at 7th Avenue North and Union Street. This happened at the same time as the name change. Yes, the show's name was changed from the WSM Barn Dance to the Grand Ole Opry. The change came about by accident. The result of an ad lib by announcer George D. Hay. Hay called himself "The Solemn Old Judge." He started the National Barn Dance on WLS in Chicago in 1924. Anyway, the WSM Barn Dance came on immediately after a broadcast of the NBC Music Appreciation Hour. An opera program conducted by Dr. Walter Damrosch. Hay opened the program by saying: "For the past hour, you've been listening to Grand Opera. Now we present Grand Ole Opry!" The name stuck.

As the live audience grew, the program moved broadcast locations several times. The first move was to a newly built studio that seated 500. Then to the Hillsboro Theatre, and next to the East Nashville Tabernacle. Another move took the Opry to the War Memorial auditorium. It seated 1200. Two years after the Opry went national, with a half hour broadcast coast to coast, it moved to the famous Ryman Auditorium where it stayed until 1974. The Ryman seats 2362.

In 1974 WSM opened an amusement Park, Opryland USA. President Nixon dedicated the park on March 16. The Opry moved into the new 15-million-dollar theatre there. It's the largest broadcasting studio in the world. It seats 4400.

The Ryman Auditorium

For over thirty years, the auditorium was known as the Union Gospel Tabernacle. It was built by a riverboat captain named Tom Ryman. Ryman's riverboats carried a large share of Nashville's River trade. His boats also had barrooms, gambling casinos, and dancing girls. He originally went to scoff and disrupt services held in downtown Nashville by Methodist revivalist Sam Jones. His visit in 1885 resulted in his conversion. Ryman, in his newfound religious zeal, cleaned up his boats. In 1889 he also financed the construction of a building where Jones and other preachers could hold revivals. After his death, the Union Gospel Tabernacle was renamed the Ryman Auditorium at the suggestion of Reverend Jones.

Recognized as one of the best concert halls in the south, with almost perfect acoustics, the auditorium continues to be used by many performers. It's still called "The Mother Church" of country music.

Who Outlawed The Fiddle And Steel Guitar?

All of that is well and good. Sadly, there's very little country music made in Nashville today. Some will argue that this goes back to the sixties, and the rise of producer Billy Sherill. Sherill's polished production style became known as the Nashville Sound. That's why legends like Waylon Jennings, Willie Nelson, and Johnny Cash were labeled outlaws. They bucked the Nashville formula.

Here's another thing that burns my biscuit. The recent, so called "CMA Awards." I'm sorry, but any show that Katy Perry or Beyonce' appears on ain't country. What's called country now is Pop, sometimes with a twang. Often, it's outright rock and roll. There is no Roy Acuff balancing his fiddle on his nose or belting out *Walkin the Floor Over You.* There's no Marty Robbins. When Marty played the Opry, he always went on last. He played until most everyone had left. Then he signed autographs and had his picture made with fans. Marty stayed until he saw them all.

The music is way different. It's electrified, over-produced and heavily Pro Tooled. So much so, the performers couldn't reproduce it on stage if they had too. Without filler tracks that is. I was going to list a bunch of those performers, but I won't. Some of you may still have some Sugarland or Luke Bryan CD's. As the great song writers Larry Cordle and Larry Shell said in the chorus of their song *Murder on Music Row*:

> "For the steel guitars no longer cry
> And the fiddles barely play
> But drums and rock 'n' roll guitars
> Are mixed up in your face
> Ol' Hank wouldn't have a chance
> On today's radio
> Since they committed murder
> Down on Music Row"

I'm purest. Give me Waylon Jennings, Willie Nelson, or Johnny Cash. Speaking of Johnny Cash, it took a genius like Rick Rubin to give him the attention he deserved near the end of his life. Willie Nelson, well he's the Keith Richards of country music. Ninety years old as I write this, and still out there. Or how about J. D. Crowe, Doyle Lawson, Del McCoury, Junior Sisk, Tim O'Brien, The Gibson Brothers, George Strait, or any number of musicians who are true to the roots. Thank God for Marty Stuart who said recently, "The most outlaw thing you can do in Nashville today is play country music." Then there's Ricky Skaggs, and Alan Jackson. Today's Music Row wouldn't know a real country musician if they saw one. It's all about formula. What formula does Merle Haggard fit? How about Ferlin Husky, Patsy Cline, and Jim Reeves? What was the trick The Louvin Brothers, or Jim and Jesse used? Can you believe I met someone the other day that didn't know who StringBean was?

I mean, really? I could go on and on, but you get the picture.

On a trip to Nashville a few years ago a group of us gathered around the old ribbon mike at the Ryman. We sang some gospel quartet-style songs. It was great fun. After a while I lost all control and sang a medley of Merle Haggard tunes. I was on cloud nine. I hope Merle will forgive me. Yeah, that's a nice, fancy concert hall you got over there on the flood plain. Give me the Ryman and the kind of music that made it famous: that's country music.

HEAVENLY BABY, HOLY CHILD

Heavenly Baby, Holy Child
Born so lowly, meek, and mild.
Precious Child, heavens best
Come to die for all the rest.

God's provision for my soul
Births foretold since days of old.
Lay so still in the cold, clear night
Come to lead us to the Light.

Baby Jesus at Mary's breast
Wise men and shepherds blessed.
The animals all stood round in awe
Calmed by everything they saw.

In that manger so long ago
My Savior came so I could know
His Father as He did; my own,
And worship Him around His throne.

Heavenly baby, Holy Child
Born so lowly, meek, and mild.
Precious Child, heavens best
Come to die for all the rest.

HIS HOLD IS LIGHT

Success is found in His grip.
His hold is light.
And there's great joy in the trip.

Life is not a destination you see.
There are twists and turns.
You never really "get there" until you're free.

Striving and stressing just makes you old.
It's not the gray hair.
In fact, gray hair should be a goal.

Each graying strand is filled with wisdom
born of experience.
Love, hate, joy, and sadness make the sum.

Time passes quickly; "poof" it's gone.
"Somebody stop this train!"
Don't strain to hear the melody and miss the song.

Remember, success is found in His grip.
His hold is light.
And there's great joy in the trip.

PAPA FREEMAN

My Papa Freeman's full name was Nathaniel Sephus Freeman. He was a mess, and for my first fifteen years my best friend. What changed? I became of driving age and bought my first car. More about that car in another chapter.

Papa Freeman's daddy was Almond Dudley Freeman. Everyone called him AD. AD was born in 1861. He was the middle child of Josephus and Elizabeth Bryan Freeman. Josephus died in spring, 1863 of meningitis just south of Fredericksburg, Virginia. He was serving in the 35th Georgia volunteers. AD's mother never remarried after Josephus' death. Elisabeth lived to be eighty-two. She died with her boots on. Again, more about Elizabeth later.

AD the boy had a tough life. It probably affected AD the man. He married Savannah Juhan in 1879. Papa was the fifth child of eight. This is a picture of AD taken not long before his murder.

The following is from an interview I did with Mr. Turner Moon in 2001. He knew AD well.

"AD was a tall slender man. He was a very good manager. He farmed and grew cotton. He was a 'cricket' of a man (able to get around very well). AD owned two farms, one of which was a four-horse farm. The home place was on Scenic Highway (GA 124) on a hill just South of Rockbridge cemetery. His first wife, Savannah, was sickly. After she died, he married Ellen Haney. Miss Haney helped him care for Savannah during her last illness. AD was very jealous of Miss Haney. One time she had in-grown toenails so bad that they had to call the doctor. He didn't want the doctor to see Ellen's legs above the ankle so they cut out the toes of her hose so he could get to them."

Almon Dudley Freeman

AD also had a dark side. Honestly, he was mean. When Savannah was dying Papa's sisters would go visit. AD kept candy in the closet. He'd ask the girls if they wanted some. Of course, they did. Savannah would ask for some too. He'd tell her no as he handed the girls their piece. Often, she'd beg but his answer was still no. One time they walked in, and Miss Haney was sitting in AD's lap. Right there in Savannah's room. Shortly after Savannah's death he and Miss Haney were wed. Papa said his mama wasn't even cold in the ground when they tied the knot. Then there was the moonshining. AD ran a groundhog style still on No-Business creek. He made Papa carry sugar to it at night. On his wedding day Papa worked in the field all morning plowing. He came in at dinner, ate, and started to clean up. AD saw him and asked him where he was going. Papa said to get married. AD said, "Not today boy. You still got plowing to do." Papa said a few choice words and left to go to his wedding. He rarely went back.

AD liked to brag. Especially about money. That led to his death. He'd been telling folks that he was going to Tucker to buy a piece of land. "I got fifteen hundred dollars cash to pay for it," he'd say. That was a lot of money in 1929. Sadly, he never made it. He was waylaid and murdered on the way. He had no will, so the estate was sold off by an administrator. The total received from the sale was twenty thousand five-hundred and thirty-two dollars. Right before the murder Papa borrowed a hoe from his daddy. That's all he got from the estate. His two living brothers got nothing either. Mrs. Haney-Freeman got it all. Here's something I found interesting. AD had a Model T Ford and mule. The Model T brought twenty-five dollars at the sale. The mule brought seventy-five! My how times have changed.

Papa and Granny married on July 29, 1906. Here's their wedding picture.

They lived in a rental house in the Lenora community for the first twenty-one years of their marriage. All five of their girls, Ila Mae, Easter Lois, Lucy Belle, Susie Marie, and Opal Jeanette were born in that house. In 1927 they bought a sixty-two-acre farm. The farm was in Centerville on Zoar Church Road. It had a three-room house, and several outbuildings. My daddy, Nathaniel Morris, was born in the "new" house on the farm. It wasn't much, but it was home. More about the land in another chapter.

Papa Freeman never had a public job. He farmed in the spring and summer. He raised cotton and wheat to sell for cash, and lots of vegetables. One day Papa was planting peas. He had an old, well used Cole single horse planter. This sophisticated implement didn't require a draft horse. A good, straight, slow-walking mule worked just fine. As I said, Papa's was old, but it was a deluxe model. It was double-potted, seed in one and fertilizer in the other. Various settings controlled the seed spacing, fertilizer output, depth, ground packing and other functions. Did I mention the machine was old? That's important. That old Cole could be temperamental. This day was one of those days. He tinkered, fiddled, and adjusted to no avail. It just wouldn't work. Thankfully Papa had already unharnessed the mule and tied him up in the shade. He let fly a stream of profanity and pitched the tool over the nearby fence. Aunt Ila Mae and Aunt Lucy were on the terrace above him hoeing beans. They both burst out laughing. That was a mistake. Papa had a little bit of a temper. Broiling sun and sweat combined with a contrary tool tended to make it flare a bit. He angrily ordered the girls to climb the fence and hand the planter back to him. They complied, and he eventually got the machine going. Mission accomplished. Peas planted.

There was a peach orchard out behind the house. Papa planted butterbeans between the trees. Every possible patch of dirt got planted. At that time, he had an old mule named Red. Red was a good mule, but he had one tiny problem. He had sensitive ears, and peach trees have limbs. Do you see the issue? Papa was ready to put in the butterbeans. He harnessed old Red and headed to the peach orchard. About halfway out the first row it happened. A peach limb brushed Red's ear, and he broke and ran. Papa, God bless him, hung on for as long as he could. Yelling "Whoa, Red. Whoa", or something like that. When he finally let go, his hat went one way, and he tumbled the other, finally crashing into a peach tree. Red stopped at the top of the hill, looked back at Papa, and snorted. That was a mistake. Papa got up, dusted himself off, retrieved his hat, and marched up the hill toward Red. When he got there, he whipped him with the trace chain and led him back to the pasture. Mules are highly intelligent animals. Some say they have the memory of an elephant. Red sure did. He never forgot the trace chain whipping. From that day on he got his revenge by stepping on Papa's foot. It happened during harnessing. Red would watch Papa's feet. When one got in the right place, he'd do the deed. Red didn't do it every time. He wanted it to appear random, an accident, if you will. I told you mules were smart.

In the late fall and winter, Papa was a finish carpenter. He had to go to Atlanta to get work. This involved rising at four o'clock in the morning, walking the one-half mile to GA-124, and hitching a ride to Lithonia. At Lithonia he'd catch the train into the city. If lucky, he'd get a job for the day. If real lucky a job might last a week, maybe more. At the end of the day, he had to reverse the trip. Often, he didn't get home till nine or ten P.M. That was when he could find work. If no work was available, he had a winter routine. He'd eat breakfast, put on his hat, and coat, and walk to Freeman's Store in Centerville. There he'd sit around the pot-bellied stove at the back of the store with the other farmers. They'd swap tall tales till dinnertime. Papa came home for dinner and then right back to Freeman's till suppertime.

On one of those winter days a local farmer came in the store. His name was Arthur Darby. Mr. Darby was a known cut-up. This day he had a can in his hand. It was made of tin and had a picture of old-fashioned peppermint candy on the outside. He said, "You want a piece of candy Seaf?" and handed the can to Papa. Papa said, "Why shore, Arthur." He reached for the can and twisted off the lid. The can didn't contain candy. It was one of those spring-loaded pop-up things. Papa jumped back and dropped the can to the floor. The other men started laughing. Papa never said a word. He just reached down and picked up the contraption, opened the door of the pot-bellied stove, and threw it in. The laughter subsided as Mr. Darby said, "Seaf, you're gonna have to pay me for that." Papa stood up, slammed the door of the stove, and said, "Are you gonna make me?" Mr. Darby sat down. The laughter returned. Papa smiled, got his coat and hat, and headed out the door for home. Mr. Darby's still waiting on his money.

Papa like to dance and have a nip of 'shine now and then. Granny was a staunch, teetotaling Baptist. Papa was a lapsed Methodist turned Baptist. He wasn't as strict as Granny. The deacons at Rock Bridge Baptist Church got wind of the dancing and sipping. They asked Papa to quit, he said "nah", and they kicked him out. He never darkened the door of the church again except for weddings and funerals. He believed in Jesus. He just didn't think Jesus had a problem with a little fun. One Saturday night Papa came in late from a dance. Granny was sitting on the front porch waiting for him. She was crying softly as she rocked in her rocking chair. Papa came up on the porch and said, "What's wrong, Maude"? Granny said not a word. She just sobbed quietly and rocked. Papa got down on his knees next to the chair. He knew what was wrong. He also knew his cavorting days were over. Papa laid his head in her lap and cried too. He loved Granny so much. It tore him up to see her cry. He never went to a dance or took a drink again. He was a changed man, and Granny never had to say a word. Her tears were enough.

My Daddy came along in 1930. It was around 1940 when Papa put a new roof on the house. During the process, as sometimes happens he missed the roofing nail and hit his thumb. He yelled, "OUCH", or something like that and flung the hammer out into the field. Daddy was playing in the yard and witnessed the toss. It stuck him as funny, laugh out loud funny. Pappa took issue with the giggles. He made Daddy go find the hammer and bring it to him. I still have that hammer.

As I said earlier, Papa was an integral part of early my life. My best buddy until I started driving. Driving led to a girlfriend (now my wife, Judy). A girlfriend led to less time at home. A teenager, with raging hormones, I didn't even realize Papa was sick. I was too busy to pay attention. Daddy called Dr. Willis McCurdy. He came to the house to see him on a Thursday night. Dr. McCurdy still made house calls in 1970. Somehow, he managed to drive to the house from Stone Mountain inebriated. He was so bad that Daddy had to help him into the house. Doc held on to the walls to get to Papa and Granny's room. At least he came. After examining Papa, he told Daddy there was nothing he could do. He needed to be in the hospital. In 1970 there was no 911. Daddy called Mr. Winston Mason. Mr. Mason's son, Miles, was a doctor. He told Daddy he'd call Miles and get back to him. A few minutes later Mr. Mason called back and told Daddy to take Papa to Joan Glancy Hospital in Duluth. Dr. Miles Mason was a founding doctor of that hospital. Dr. Mason admitted Papa and started tests and treatment.

By now it was early Friday morning. By Saturday afternoon he was better. I went to the football game Friday night. I was busy Saturday. Then came Sunday. Sunday Papa left this mortal coil. He died of kidney failure. I never went to see him in the hospital. I could have. I should have, but I didn't. I have few regrets in this life. Not visiting Papa as he lay dying is my biggest one. I think about him every day, and yes, I still miss him. I told him I was sorry at the funeral home. I told him again at the funeral, and at the graveside.

Today I live within sight of where his mortal remains lie. I know he forgave me a long time ago. He loved my girlfriend who's now my wife. I'll see you soon Papa. When I get there don't ask me to pull your finger. I'm on to your trickery.

PAPA'S CHAIR

I still have Papa's chair.
It's been re-covered, but it's still his.
When I sit in it, I can feel his presence.
The memories of him pour in like a flood, and
I let them carry me away.

Papa loved "Live Atlanta Wrestling."
He thought it was real.
Dick the Bruiser, and the Assassins
were his companions every Saturday night.
Two falls, or a TV time limit.

And the wisdom he dispensed from that chair.
"Get your books." he'd say,
and I knew to study hard.
"Boy, you'd tear up the Iron Devil."
Be careful son, things break.

Papa was quick with a joke.
He knew a million of them.
Those he called "smutty tales"
were mild by today's standards.
I'd love to hear him tell one now.

I still have Papa's chair.
If that was all I had I'd be sad.
But I have much, much more.
I have his memories,
and I'll never re-cover those.

JUDY'S CREAM CHEESE POUND CAKE

Ingredients

- 3 cups butter (softened)
- 1 package (8 ounce) cream cheese
- 3 cups sugar
- 6 eggs
- 1 1/2 teaspoon vanilla
- 3 cups Martha White All Purpose flour
- 1/4 teaspoon salt

Instructions

1. Preheat oven to 350-degrees.
2. Grease and flour bottom and sides of a 10-inch tube pan.

3. In a large bowl, beat butter and cream cheese on medium speed until well mixed.

4. Add sugar; beat until light and fluffy.

5. Add eggs, one at a time, beating well after each addition.

6. Beat in vanilla. Spoon flour into measuring cup; level off. Add flour and salt. Beat just until mixed.

7. Spoon batter into greased pan.

8. Place in 350-degree oven for 1 hour 35 minutes to 1 hour and 45 minutes or until toothpick inserted 1 inch from edge comes out clean.

9. Cool in pan 5 minutes.

10. Turn out onto wire rack and cool completely.

Eat plain, or serve with fresh fruit, if desired.
Store in refrigerator.

POLITICIANS
ARE LIARS

I was just thinking, and sometimes that's painful. I know that thinking is painful for some of you too. Anyway, in the land of unsocial media, it's easier just to repost someone else's rant. Heaven forbid that you'd have to think a little and develop your own thoughts. Really, I get it, but I digress.

Let's talk about politicians. No really, let's. Folks these people are, for the most part, habitual, natural-born liars. As Papa Freeman used to say, "They'd rather climb a tree to tell a lie when they can tell the truth standing on the ground". Why do you seem so surprised that our current bunch are lying to us? They're just doing what politicians do. And the media, some of you call it "mainstream media". You get your knickers in a twist because they're biased. Tellers of tales lie. They reorganize the facts to fit their predisposition. When that doesn't work, they make up facts of their own, also known as lies. This is nothing new. Human beings are biased.

Bias is ever present since the dawn of the printing press. Back then press equipment cost a fortune. This limited the ownership of the printing press to the wealthy and powerful. Guess what? They slanted what they printed to serve their interests. Sound familiar? Murdoch, Turner, Hearst, and Pulitzer come to mind. Heck, take old Ben Franklin, for instance. In colonial times, newspapers had little news. They were mainly made up of advertisements. Property and farms for sale, and runaway slaves. As the American Revolution began, both Franklin and the and the British used the press to support their bias. British pamphlets discredited the patriots. Franklin, and other colonial printers, pushed for freedom from British rule while vilifying parliament and King George.

Once the war began, Franklin and others used the press to keep patriot colonists engaged. Even when battles happened in distant locations across the country. Over 30 weekly newspapers existed at the beginning of the Revolution. These papers exchanged stories. In doing so, the same information reached other cities. Newspapers helped unify the fragile thirteen colonies. They treated readers as one large community. This helped the colonies support each other during the Revolution.

Fast forward to just before the turn of the nineteenth century. The young country became politically split between the Jeffersonian Republicans and the Madison, Hamilton, and Jay led Federalists. The press split along the same lines. Partisan in the vilest way. Name calling was commonplace, as was outright lies. Jefferson and John Adams, best of friends, became enemies due to the lies spread by newspapers. Thankfully, they reconciled in 1812. They died on July 4, 1826. Adams last words were, "Thomas Jefferson still lives." Sadly, Jefferson died that morning. Adams died in the evening.

Let's take a short stroll through recent history. Bill Clinton lied when he said he didn't have sex with Monica Lewinsky. Ronald Reagan lied about involvement in Iran-Contra. Richard Nixon lied when he said he didn't know anything about the Watergate break in. Lyndon Johnson lied about the Gulf of Tonkin incident so he could begin the Vietnam war in earnest. John Kennedy lied about US nuclear missiles in Turkey during the Cuban missile crisis. Franklin Roosevelt lied about the Yalta Agreement. You know, the agreement that "gave" Eastern Europe to the Soviets after World War II. G. W. Bush lied about weapons of mass destruction. Obama lied when he said on

The Tonight Show, "There is no spying on Americans". Trump lied when he denied knowing about the hush money paid to Stormy Daniels. I only selected one lie of the many they told. They were all presidents. Try not to think about the hundreds of other politicians that lied yesterday, are lying today, and will lie tomorrow. Sickening, isn't it?

What about the biggest liar of the last 100 years, Adolf Hitler? He and his propaganda minster, Joseph Goebbels, used the "big lie" to turn a nation of antisemitic leaning people into a nation capable of mass murder. Hitler and Goebbels told lies about Jews. Huge, unbelievable lies. They told them often. Lies so big and so unbelievable they had to be true. No one could possibly make something up that was so fantastic. The "big lie" theory at work equals the ashes of over 6 million people.

Yep. Politicians are liars. Past, present, and future. It will all be different however, as the late Johnny Cash said, "...when the Man comes around".

GLACIER POINT AT SUNSET

I stood on Glacier Point at sunset,
as shadows slowly crawled up Half Dome.
They rolled over the tops of the peaks,
and spilled onto the valley floor.
Yosemite at eventide.
Your presence is everywhere.
Time slows down as nature speaks.

Alpenglow's pinkish hue
is painted across the Sierra Nevada.
The setting sun has done this.
In the quiet of the moment
I hear the twin falls, Nevada and Vernal.
Their water that once was snow
crashes to the rocks with a muffled roar.

Though people are all around me
I am alone with my thoughts.
It's hard to breathe.
Is it the altitude, or the glory of Your creation
that's ever changing before my eyes?
Glacier Point at sunset
is a magical, mystical place.
I never want to leave.

IT'S "POTLIKKER" Y'ALL

In 1982 the late Zell Miller wrote the following to The New York Times. "Dear Sir: I always thought The New York Times knew everything ... Only a culinarily-illiterate damnyankee (one word) who can't tell the difference between beans and greens would call the liquid left in the pot after cooking greens 'pot liquor' (two words) instead of 'potlikker' (one word) as yours did. And don't cite Webster as a defense because he didn't know any better either. Sincerely, Zell Miller, Lieutenant Governor State of Georgia."

The offending article ran February 23, 1982, Section A, Page 18. It wasn't a food review. In fact, the piece wasn't about food at all. It was about Huey Long. It seems the late senator from Louisiana, led a filibuster in 1935. Long opposed President Franklin D. Roosevelt's New Deal. His stated goal was to force Senate confirmation of the National Recovery Administration's leadership. His real goal was personal. He wanted to keep political enemies in Louisiana from cushy NRA jobs. Senator Long spoke for 15 hours and 30 minutes, at that time the second longest Senate filibuster ever. He read and pontificated on the U.S. Constitution. He claimed the president's programs transformed the Constitution into "ancient and forgotten lore." He also lectured his colleagues on the merits of potlikker. Finally, at 4 a.m., Senator Long was overcome by the call of nature and yielded the floor. The Times reporter didn't believe that potlikker was a word and consulted a dictionary. Thus, he referred to the Southern delicacy as "pot liquor."

Old Zell, before politics got in his blood, was a teacher. His subject was history. A good Methodist, he taught at Young Harris College, a Methodist school in northeast Georgia. Miller saw the faux pas and was compelled to educate. He knew that potlikker is the liquid left after boiling a mess of greens. Greens such as mustard, turnip, beet tops, collards, or if you lived way out in country poke salad. Your greens of choice must be seasoned with ham hocks or salt pork and salt and pepper. The 'likker is full of vitamins, calcium, and a little grit if the greens ain't washed properly. Old timers say, among other things, that potlikker keeps a child's legs straight. No one wants their child to be knock-kneed or bowlegged.

Granny Freeman put the juice in the ice box. She later transitioned to a refrigerator. She drank it for breakfast. Sometimes she made soup with potlikker. She'd pour it into a pot, add some water, whatever meat and vegetables she had leftover, and some home canned tomatoes (see the chapter *The Tomato Incident*). When the soup was ready, she placed a good helping in a bowl. Then she'd crumble some fresh, cast-iron skillet baked cornbread into the soup. A meal fit for a king. Granny said a starving person could survive by licking the pot. She also believed that doses of potlikker and bone marrow broth were a curative for women. Especially one taken to bed after childbirth. Or one whose husband ran off with the church secretary. Either way, it worked miracles.

Potlikker affects folks in strange ways. For instance, I know of a sad case between a mother and child. It seems the mother asked the child to water her plants. She came home and found that the child threw away two of her 30 Mason jars of rooting begonias. Nothing was ever said about the transgression. Another time said child went into her pantry and threw away some canned goods. Just the several that were years beyond the "use by" date. Again, the mother said not a word. Ah, but the time the child came into the kitchen to help clean up and threw away the brown-green juice in the bottom of the pots. It was as if the unpardonable sin was committed. "What's the matter with you?" she shrieked. "Are you plain crazy? You don't throw away potlikker. Never. Not ever. You hear?!"

Wasting potlikker is just not allowed. Anyone who does is a no account. A distant uncle on my mother's side was a truck driver. He hauled chickens to a processing plant near Birmingham, Alabama. On the return trip he'd haul a load of nut's, bolts, screws, and washers from Birmingham Fastener to Atlanta. On one of these trips, he met a woman at a truck stop. She was a bleached blonde with long hot-pink fingernails. For some reason he thought it was a good idea to bring her home and set up housekeeping. Grandmother Attaway went over to meet her. As was her custom, she brought a welcoming pound cake. Upon her arrival at the backdoor, she saw the hussy had made a pot of greens. However, to Grandmothers horror, she had thrown the potlikker through the screen door. It was still running down the screen and dripping onto the top step. Grandmother was furious. Within a week, the woman and all her belongings were on the Greyhound out of town. My uncle refused to sleep in their bed. He boo-hooed himself to sleep on the couch. You didn't mess with Grandmother Attaway.

A typical welcome at a Southern home goes something like this: "Come on in... Push the door to... Make yourself at home... I already boiled the pot." A good woman always keeps a cast-iron skillet of cornbread in the oven. And a boiled pot of greens on the stove. She's always ready for company or a stranger. Listen, don't think potlikker is the same as the stuff at the bottom of percolated coffee or scuppernong wine. That's the "dregs". Dregs can be thrown through the screen door or disposed of at the edge of the yard. City folk may even put them on a compost pile.

Potlikker and people are a lot alike. Some folks are like boiling water that stays on too long. This results from the many speed bumps of life. Things like whippings with a switch that leave a scar. A couple of kissing cousins going too far. Abandonment by a parent or parents. Learning to read at the age of four, then dropping out of school. Cooties. Then there's car and bank crashes. The list goes on; broken bones, bankruptcy, impacted teeth, dropsy, a bad marriage, eviction, filmy eyes, rheumatism, epizootic in your cows, ringing in the ears, gout, collapsed lung and roof, grippe, consumption, runaway child, apoplexy, blind staggers, hookworms, hardening of the arteries, hysterics, weak constitution, typhoid, fits, droughts, the runs, boils, stones in the kidney, enlarged hearts, stillborn babies, an angry uterus, suffocation by cats, a dry well, case of the nerves, lumbago, and lingering death, just to name a few. Even with all of this, or more, some folks still find it within themselves to be kind to everyone they meet.

In the South when folks pass on, neighbors bring food to the house. When my mom passed, our church covered us with food. Way more than the two of us could eat. A friend of the family, Thomas Livsey, called to offer his condolences. He said, "Brother Freeman, is there anything y'all need?" I replied that we had more than plenty, and that his call was enough. That evening I heard a horn blow. I looked out the window to see who it was. There was Thomas' beige Town Car in the driveway. I went out to see him. He's ninety years old and doesn't get around very well. He popped the trunk. He'd brought fried chicken, green beans, macaroni-and-cheese (considered a vegetable in the South), biscuits, and a banana pudding. I thanked him and carried the bounty inside. We ate the banana pudding and froze most of the rest. This meal was entered into our meal rotation. Good eating for the next six months.

Sadly, some folks cross the threshold without many friends,

and sometimes no family. We give them the benefit of the doubt. We're sure they were a good soul. It doesn't matter that the preacher doesn't know the person. He reads the 23rd Psalm anyway. Its verses promise they'll lay down in green pastures, not on hard clods of red clay. Granny Freeman said that what's left in the bottom of the pot, the potlikker, is the green's real value. And after all, when people die, it's the memories of them that are passed on to others. Sort of like the memory of the greens left in the potlikker.

GRANNY FREEMAN'S MEATLOAF

Ingredients

- 1 pound ground beef
- 1 cup onions, chopped
- ¼ cup bell pepper, chopped
- 1 teaspoon salt
- ½ teaspoon pepper
- 2 eggs
- 10-12 crackers, crushed
- 1/2 cup catsup
- ½ cup water

Instructions

1. Preheat oven to 400 degrees Fahrenheit.

2. Mix catsup and water until well blended. Set aside.

3. Mix ground beef, onion, bell pepper salt, pepper eggs, ½ of catsup/water mixture and crackers in a bowl until thoroughly blended. This is best done by hand. Wash them first!

4. Place mixture into loaf pan and place in oven.

5. Bake for 30 minutes, after 15 minutes spread rest of catsup/water mixture on top, and place back into oven for the last 15 minutes.

SPRING

I took a walk in the warmth of the sun,
and as I looked around, I saw work to be done.
I sensed that Old Man Winter had let us slip from his hold.
He was back in the Arctic where it's always cold.

There were shrubs to be trimmed and flower beds to weed.
The patchy front lawn needed some seed.
Tree limbs lay willy-nilly around all about.
Yes, there was work to be done I had no doubt.

So, I rolled up my sleeves and attacked all the tasks.
One by one they were finished till I came to the last,
and I finished it too, not being one to quit.
Then I looked all around. Good work: I was so proud of it.

I took a walk in the warmth of the sun,
and when I looked around there was no work to be done.

PIGS SMELL BETTER COOKED

I love barbeque. Some will say I'm obsessed with it. I've driven miles out of my way to eat barbeque. In another life I traveled the state of Georgia as part of my job. I ate a lot of barbeque. If there was a pig farmer in a town, he had problems with his hogs when I came through. The swine could sense my presence and they squealed and trembled, but I digress. All the above makes me an expert on Georgia barbeque. So, why am I sharing the results of my years of research? It would be a disservice to humanity not to do so. It would also be a disgrace to my Southern heritage. Therefore, I am compelled to share my research with you dear reader.

What is barbeque? That is the question, isn't it? Well to be sure we get started off on the right foot let me answer that question. When we're talking barbeque, we're talking slow cooked pork. If properly prepared no sauce is necessary. It's not always the case, but poorly prepared meat is sometimes covered in sauce to hide its badness. A despicable practice, but it happens. No beef, no bison, or any other strange or exotic meat is barbeque. It can be barbequed, but that don't make it barbeque. For those of us from the deep South barbeque is pork-pig, thank you very much. This is our distinctly Southern definition of the word. One that won't be found in dictionaries. It's also a very broad definition. It represents many different styles and flavors as you travel across "The Barbeque Belt". John Shelton Reed in his seminal book *Holy Smoke: The Big Book of North Carolina*

Barbeque (2008, The University of North Carolina Press) put it simply, "Southern barbeque is the closest thing we have in the United States to Europe's wines or cheeses; drive a hundred miles and the barbeque changes."

The culinary topography of The Barbeque Belt is sauce driven. It begins with the peppered vinegar-based sauces of Eastern North Carolina. The sauces brighten with the addition of tomato as you move west across the state. South Carolina is known for its mustard-based sauces. Georgia adds hot orange and sweet red sauces to the mix. Alabama throws in a little mayonnaise for its unique white sauce. Tennessee rounds out the mix with its sweet, thick tomato/molasses sauce. You'll find all these styles and some unique ones in Georgia.

Also, I mention barbeque joints by name in this chapter. They got mentioned by meeting four simple criteria:

1. They must provide great barbeque as defined above.
2. The original owner or a descendent must be dripping some sweat into the sauce, so to speak.
3. There must be a story, and
4. I must like it enough to go back.

It's as simple as that. I hope you enjoy your research half as much as I did mine.

A Brief History Of Barbeque

I would be remiss if I didn't provide some intellectual stimulation. This brief history of barbeque is meant to do that. It is by no means complete.

The Origin Of The Word "Barbeque"

The roads of most other Southern states are lined with

barbeque signs. Most bear a grinning pig advertising barbeque for sale. The origins of barbeque in the South are traceable. Barbeque was around long before the smiling pig became a fixture on Southern roadsides. The origin of the term "barbeque" is vague. The most credible theory says that the word "barbeque" or "barbecue" springs from the West Indian word "barbacoa." This word is used to describe slow-cooking meat over hot coals. *Bon Appetit* magazine informs its readers that the word comes from an extinct tribe in Guyana. These natives enjoyed "cheerfully spit-roasting captured enemies." *The Oxford English Dictionary* says the word is Haitian. Some claim (somewhat improbably) that "barbeque" is French. The French phrase is *"barbe a queue"* meaning "from head to tail." Fans of this theory point to smoking the whole hog as some cooks do. I like this one from *Tar Heel* magazine. They say that the word "barbeque" comes from a 19th advertisement. The ad was for a combination whiskey bar, beer hall, pool hall, and seller of smoked pig. The joint was known as the **BAR-BEER-CUE-PIG**. The most rational notion is that roasting meat over powdery coals was picked up from indigenous peoples in the colonial period. The word "barbacoa" that describes this way of cooking became "barbeque" in the lexicon of early settlers.

Antebellum Barbeque

For several reasons the pig became a food staple in the South. Pigs were a low-maintenance and convenient food source. In the pre-Civil War period Southerners ate, on average, five pounds of pork for every one pound of beef (Gray 27). The hog was easy to keep. Pigs could be put out to root in the forest and caught when needed. These semi-wild pigs were tougher and stringier than modern hogs. Every part of the pig was used. The meat was either eaten immediately or cured for later. The ears, organs and other parts were also eaten. "Hog Killing Time" was in the late fall and became a celebration. Neighbors were invited to share in the bounty. The traditional Southern barbeque grew out of these gatherings.

By the end of the colonial period the practice of barbeques was well established. It was in the fifty years before the Civil War that the traditions associated with large barbeques became deep-rooted. Plantation owners regularly held large and festive barbeques. These sometimes included "pig pickin's" for slaves (Hilliard 59). In the antebellum period pork production became a matter of Southern patriotism. Very little of the pork produced left the South. Raising pigs made for a self-sufficient food supply. Southern pork for Southern people if you will. (Hilliard 99). Hogs became fatter and better cared-for. (*The History of Barbecue - University of Virginia*") Farmers began to feed them corn to fatten them up. The stringy and tough wild pigs became well-fed domesticated hogs. Barbeque was only one facet of pork production, but more hogs meant more barbeques.

Mixing Politics And Religion

In the 19th century, barbeque was a staple at church picnics, political rallies, and private parties (Egerton 150). A barbeque was a popular and relatively inexpensive way to lobby for votes. The organizers of political rallies would provide barbeque, lemonade, sweet tea, and usually whiskey (Bass 307). A father and son team of Georgia politicians made political rallies featuring barbeque famous. I'm referring to Eugene Talmadge and his son Herman. According to my grandfather they provided whiskey too, often in copious amounts. These gatherings were also an easy way for different classes to mix. Barbeque wasn't a class-specific food. Large groups of people from every level of society could come together to eat, drink, and listen to stump speeches. Church barbeques, where roasted pig supplemented the covered dishes prepared by the ladies of the congregation, were a part of the traditional church picnic in many Southern communities. Church and political barbeques are still a vital tradition in many parts of the South (Bass 301).

The "Secret Society" Of Pit Men

My grandfather, Robert Attaway aka Daddy Bob, was the pit man for the Masonic lodges in the Atlanta area. If a lodge was planning a barbeque fund raiser, they called on him. This picture on the following page was taken at Grant Park in Atlanta, Georgia around 1956. He and his team cooked for two days.

They smoked over five thousand pork shoulders and butts. He also made ten ninety-gallon cauldrons of Brunswick Stew. The stew was simmered over an open fire and had to be stirred constantly to keep it from sticking. They stirred it with boat paddles. My cousin, Danny Attaway, continues the tradition. He oversees the annual barbeque at the Stone Mountain Masonic Lodge.

The success of barbeque at political rallies and church picnics led to barbeque restaurants. They grew out of a simple barbeque pit where the owner sold barbeque to take away. Many only opened on Saturday. The pit men worked (usually on a farm) during the week, tended the pit on Friday night, and sold the barbeque on Saturday. The typical barbeque shack had a bare concrete floor surrounded by a corrugated tin roof and walls (Johnson 9). Some even had dirt floors covered in sawdust. Soon, stools and tables were added. It wouldn't be long before the ever-present smiling pig showed up on the outside of the building. Pit men owned one restaurant. Cooking the pig required almost constant attention. The sauce and how to make it became a closely guarded secret. Very few pit men shared the secrets of their sauce. Daddy Bob was one who wouldn't share his recipe.

Georgia Barbeque

As stated earlier, Georgia barbeque is pork. It's slow cooked over an open pit stoked with oak and/or hickory wood. Although good barbeque is best eaten sauceless, we find a variety of sauces depending on where the meat is smoked. The most popular sauce is based on ketchup, molasses, bourbon, garlic, cayenne pepper, and other ingredients. However, the reality is that barbeque culture in Georgia is diverse. We have a range of styles, traditions, and influences. As such, Georgia is a melting pot of regional variations. Almost any sauce or cooking style can be found.

Barbeque in the Eastern part of the state (from St. Simons Island to Augusta) is unusual. It consists of finely chopped pork, usually shoulder or ham. It's served with a side of hash (a thick, tomato-based stew flavored with meat drippings and vegetables) over long grain white rice. Occasionally, ribs, chicken, and/or beef brisket are also on the menu. All meats are slow cooked "bare" (without spice rubs or sauces) over wood coals. All meats are served with the afore mentioned "hash and rice" and sweet pickles. Mustard-based potato salad or traditional mayonnaise-dressing coleslaw completes the meal. Many of the most famous east Georgia joints have nothing else on the menu. Typical sauces found in east Georgia are ketchup and/or vinegar based. Some include exotic flavors like

Worcestershire sauce, bay leaves, honey, and even clove. Here's a great, east Georgia barbeque joint, Sconyers.

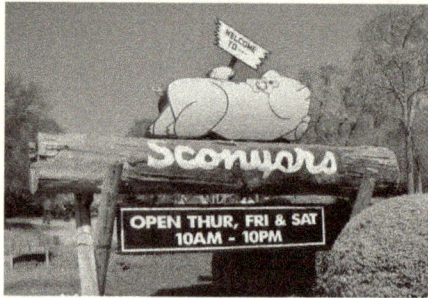

Sconyers Bar-B-Que was founded in 1956 when farming stopped being profitable for the Sconyers family. Claude and Adeline Sconyers had cooked barbeque for years. They decided to turn their hobby into a business. They opened a small shack on Peach Orchard Road in Augusta. The restaurant became popular with locals. Many came to enjoy pork barbeque and hash cooked to perfection. The family policy is simple: quality food, prepared well, served in generous portions at a fair price. Despite their success Claude and Adeline could never have imagined the ultimate success of the business they started. Larry Sconyers, Claude, and Adeline's youngest son took over the business when Claude died. Under Larry the business became a force in the Augusta area. He moved the restaurant to a new location and increased seating capacity. He also expanded into catering. Over the years Sconyers' Bar-B-Que was served on the White House lawn for President Jimmy Carter and members of Congress. It's also been served in Atlanta at the Georgia Capital, as well as many other local and state events.

Sconyer's is still family owned. They continue to follow Claude and Adeline's founding principle: quality food, prepared well, served in generous portions at a fair price. The menu still has pork barbeque and hash. Now you'll also find tenderloin, beef, chicken, and turkey with all the traditional fixings. I love the banana pudding. Yes, I eat a bowl after gorging myself on the barbeque. If you're ever over in the CSRA (Central Savannah River Area) give Sconyers a try. They never disappoint.

Sconyers is open Thursday, Friday, Saturday from 10:00 AM to 9:00 PM, They're located at 2250 Sconyers Way, Augusta, GA 30906

Middle Georgia barbeque restaurants (from Macon to Atlanta) serve Brunswick Stew instead of hash. They offer more side choices. You'll find French fries, onion rings, baked beans, and potato chips on the menu. The meat in "middle Georgia barbeque" is primarily pork, but there is diversity. Restaurants here regularly offer beef brisket, ribs, chicken, and sometimes smoked sausage. They all feature traditional shoulder-cut chopped pork. Sauces can lean to "bourbon and ketchup" based styles. My favorite middle Georgia joint, Fresh Air Bar-B-Que, serves a vinegar ketchup sauce that they've used since the 1940's,

My mouth is watering as I write these words. There's something about a barbeque joint with sawdust floors even if they're on the porch. Fresh Air Bar-B-Que in Jackson, Georgia is one of those places. It's the barbeque joint by which all others in Georgia are measured.

Dr. Joel Watkins, a Jackson veterinarian and bachelor, started Fresh Air in late 1928. He served his first "que" in 1929. Later he leased the restaurant to George W. "Toots" Caston of Jackson. "Toots" ran the restaurant until the death of Dr.

Watkins in 1945. He then borrowed $1500.00 and went into the barbeque business for himself.

Toots began working on improvements. He developed his own sauce recipe, enhanced the cooking methods, and fine-tuned his father's recipe for Brunswick Stew. Toots made Fresh Air Bar-B-Que well known all over the state. It became a favorite stopping off point on the road between Macon and Atlanta before I-75. Traffic and growth led to an enclosed dining room and indoor restrooms in 1956. The location just north of Indian Springs State Park was and is a good one. It became a favorite of Georgia Governors including Eugene Talmadge, his son Herman Talmadge, Joe Frank Harris, and Sonny Perdue.

Many believers who traveled to the famous camp meetings at Indian Springs Holiness Campground ate at Fresh Air. These old time Pentecostals came to reconciliation within themselves between the Law and Grace. Their spiritual awakening spelled doom for many porkers over the years. Amen, and pass the light bread please.

Later, Toots two daughters, Charlotte Caston Barber and Ellen Caston Brewer joined the business. In 1966 Ellen's husband Jim Brewer joined Fresh Air as manager. Jim is now managing partner.

Fresh Air is a great place to eat, and not just because they have great barbeque. The main building looks like it came from the movie set of *"The Grapes of Wrath"*. If you're standing in the parking lot facing the buildings, the one on the left is the old restaurant. The new one on the right is built of rough, darkly stained wood. Smoke billows from the chimney. Sawdust covers the floor on the porch outside. Inside long wooden tables stretch out like a rustic cafeteria. Downstairs is a large room that seats a hundred or more. The bathrooms are a little rough. They never take the graffiti off so if you're an "outhouse poet" there's no place to pontificate.

At Fresh Air they cook differently than many BBQ joints. Here's what I mean. Most use cookers and gas to cook with and use some wood to smoke with. Fresh Air does all their cooking with wood. It's a painstaking process that takes 18 to 24 hours. They use ham and only ham, always have. Ham retains more moisture than a pig shoulder or a Boston butt. A shoulder or Boston butt weighs 5 to 6 pounds and a ham is 15 to 20 pounds. This size difference is another reason cooking takes longer. The yield is better from a ham and has less fat content. If you care, and I don't, ham makes healthier barbeque. I can't believe I just wrote that.

The food at Fresh Air is simple. That's how I like it. A barbeque plate comes with barbeque, Brunswick Stew, light bread (you Northern folks call it white bread), slaw, and soda crackers (saltines my Yankee friends). Years ago, they just put a loaf of light bread on the table, and you ate what you wanted. After a health inspector had a stroke over this, they went to two pieces wrapped in wax paper. I guess that's what some folks call progress. You can get a sandwich and chips but give me the plate. As I said earlier, they use the same vinegar ketchup sauce "Toots" created in the 1940's. Some would call it North Carolina style, but the flavor and consistency are not the same.

Fresh Air Bar-B-Que is open 7 days a week for lunch and dinner. It's located at 1164 Highway 42 S, Jackson (Flovilla), Georgia 30233

I may have to rethink this butt thing. Ham healthy, ham healthy, ham healthy...

Northeast Georgia barbeque is centered around the city of Athens and its neighboring counties. It also extends northeastward along Interstate 85 into South Carolina. Northeast Georgia barbeque is like barbeque found in western South Carolina. Most restaurants in the region serve more finely chopped pork. They use a slow roasted whole hog, rather than just a pork shoulder. Meat is served with a thinner, vinegar-based sauce, and pulled pork sandwiches are especially popular. Bar H in Franklin Springs (Royston) is a great example.

Bar H is owned by the father-son team of Brian and Barkley Hart. They've been drawing crowds to a converted house in Franklin Springs for over 23 years. Franklin Springs is about 10 minutes off I-85 in Franklin County, near Royston. I dream about Bar H. The Harts hickory-and-pecan smoke their pork. The soupy, finely ground pork and beef "stew," and the wonderful coleslaw.

Eating there reminds me of my childhood. I grew up in the country. We didn't eat out much. When we did, it was a big deal. Bar H is like that. It's not an everyday thing. They're only open Thursday through Saturday. Can you say, "road trip".

The last time I was at Bar H I got to chat with Barkley Hart. I asked him about planning how much to cook. His answer was classic, "We cook what we think we can sell that day, and when we're out, we're out".

Sure, you can get smoked chicken, tender baby back ribs and spareribs. I go for a pork plate, with stew and slaw every time. Make sure to take a little bit of each with every bite. Me, I just mix it together. And, just as your stew runs out, a server shows up. They have a pitcher with stew. They ask you if you want a refill. Yes, please!

House made Southern layer cakes and pies are right by the cash register. You'll get a chance to partake before you check out. The proximity to the exit is sort of a last temptation, and I've taken home a piece quite often. You'll see kids going for the bright pink strawberry layer cake. I liked it too. The Bar H chocolate meringue pie reminds me of my mothers.

Bar H is open Thursday, Friday, Saturday from 10:00 AM to 9:00 PM. They're located at 1380 Franklin Springs Street, Royston, Georgia.

West Georgia barbeque is centered in the city of Columbus. Barbeque there is like Alabama-style barbeque. Restaurants typically serve mustard and vinegar-based sauces. And the sauces often feature jalapenos or other hot peppers. Meats in West Georgia barbeque are typically cooked over oak (particularly White Oak) coals. Barbeque here is served with dill (rather than sweet) pickles. Sometimes you'll find grilled slices of Vidalia onion. The West Georgia style also features the greatest variety of side dishes. Country vegetables such as sweet potatoes, collard greens, lima beans, mac-and-cheese (yes down here mac-and-cheese is a vegetable) and corn. West Georgia barbeque is often served with cornbread. White "loaf" bread is still common too. I like Sprayberry's Barbeque in Newnan.

Sprayberry's Barbeque started out as Houston Sprayberry's gas station on Highway 29 just north of downtown Newnan. By 1926, Houston was selling enough barbeque sandwiches to close the pumps. A barbeque joint was born. With his sauce and wife Mattie Lou's Brunswick Stew, Sprayberry's Barbeque was off and running.

Four generations of the Sprayberry family have run the joint for almost ninety-seven years. Travelers, businessmen, and locals have embraced their barbeque. Politicians of all stripes campaign at Sprayberry's. Entertainers and athletes stop in for barbeque. Regular customers also include football fans from Athens, Atlanta, and Auburn. Others visit as they travel to and from the Gulf coast, or "Redneck Rivera." Families have made Sprayberry's a holiday tradition. Country music's Alan Jackson used to work there. He waited tables during high school. When he's home he stops in for his barbecue, Brunswick Stew, and lemon pie. The late humorist, Lewis Grizzard, called Sprayberry's, "merely the best barbeque joint on earth." They serve a Lewis Grizzard Special in his memory. That's a barbecue sandwich, Brunswick Stew, and onion rings.

It's a pork plate and sweet tea for me. Pork comes sliced or pulled. I order mine pulled. They serve their meat slathered in sauce. That's not usually a good sign. My first time there, I dug around a bit and found a piece in its natural state. It was very good. Not dry like I expected. It was tender and smoky. The sauce is slightly hot. The sides were quite nice. The sweet and sour coleslaw is different. It's something I think I'd have to develop a taste for. The Brunswick Stew is slow-cooked and very tasty. The dill pickles on the side were a surprise. My plate also came with the Southerner's requisite light bread (3 pieces). Another surprise: a side of extra sauce for dipping.

Everyone that comes through the door knows one or more of their fellow diners. They're like a large family having dinner together. The service is excellent and very friendly.

Sprayberry's is open every day from 10:30 AM to 9:00 PM, except Sunday. They're located at 229 Jackson Street Newnan, Georgia 30263

That leaves a couple of regions, and the Atlanta metro area. I don't really have a favorite in North or South Georgia. There are a lot of fine joints in both regions. One to avoid is Jimbo's Log Kitchen in Homerville Georgia. Jimbo's meets all the criteria for a great joint. Their meats are great, but it's their Brunswick Stew. I'm sorry, but they put butter beans in their stew. Who does that? Barbeque in North Georgia, particularly those counties around Chattanooga share many traits with the "smokey" Tennessee style. South Georgia Barbeque, centered in and around Albany, Thomasville and Valdosta, shares qualities with its North Florida neighbors. The South Georgia folks use dry spice rubs and a hickory wood smoke for cooking.

Atlanta is the poster child for the reputation of Georgia as a "melting pot" of barbeque styles. Virtually every style found in the state is found here. You'll also find styles typical of Kansas City, Saint Louis, Texas, Chicago, Korea, and the Caribbean. These are not only present but commonplace. Forgive me, but I'm about to wax nostalgic. I can't talk about Atlanta barbeque without talking about Harold's Barbeque. Harold's had a long run, sixty-five years. Sadly, they served their last crackling cornbread on Thursday May 3, 2012.

Harold's Barbeque was an Atlanta institution near an institution, the Atlanta Federal Penitentiary. It was the safest place to eat in the city of Atlanta. At dinner and supper, the place was full of law enforcement from all jurisdictions: Federal, State, and Local. You were more likely to have trouble in Buckhead. There was so much to love about the relic that was Harold's.

The joint opened in 1947. The original owner was Harold Hembree, Jr. Mr. Hembree passed away in 2008. That was the beginning of the end of the Atlanta legend. Here is a quick breakdown of why I loved Harold's:

1. They never left the neighborhood, period. If you've never been you'll see what I mean. The skittish in your group lock the doors and sit low in the seat when you got close.

2. The cinder block old, exposed grill and the greasy charred spit in the backroom.

3. The way the whole place smelled like smoked meat. If you had lunch at Harold's, you couldn't lie about it when you got home. The evidence emanated from you.

4. The interior décor was early mobile home. The wood paneling had darkened to a rich brown patina. Probably from years of cigarette and barbeque smoke. The table sets and bar were from the late 50's.

5. The food was good. I mean really good.

The staff loved the food and the people they served. As I've described the place wasn't much to look at so good food and good service kept folks coming back.

Harold's was known for their pulled pork sandwich. Why? It was a winner. The bread was plain loaf bread (white) toasted on an old wire grate over fresh, red-hot coals. The pork was tender and the sauces good. They had two, house made: mild and hot. The mild was a thin, North Carolina tangy vinegar-based sauce. The hot tasted almost exactly like a thicker Red Rooster hot sauce. You could get a pork plate sliced or chopped. You could also get bark, the burned outer portions, mixed in the meat. The pork plate came with a generous portion of meat, a mayo-based slaw, a bowl of their famous Brunswick Stew and 2 large pieces of corn bread atop a handful of potato chips. The pork came naked. No sauce, which you know I appreciate. The meat was juicy, tender and had a nice smokey flavor. Let's not forget the sweet, iced tea and the fountain drinks. Both served in squishy Styrofoam cups with tiny, crushed ice. Reminded me of being a kid for some reason.

Now, let's talk about their cornbread. Harold's cornbread was cracklin' cornbread. It was mighty fine. I once took a Scottish friend of mine there for dinner. He asked me what the crunchy bits were in the bread. I told him that a man from a country that eats Haggis shouldn't be asking questions. My Yankee friends can Google cracklin's. I wouldn't tell Martin, and I ain't telling you. See the chapter, *Hog Killing Time* if you must know.

Harold's was not only a restaurant it was an experience. Here's my favorite Harold's happening. My coworkers and I went to Harold's for dinner a couple of times a month. This day we were in the back room. We heard someone at the counter getting rowdy with the man behind the register. The customer pulled a pistol and laid it on the Formica counter. The cashier pulled his pistol out and laid it on the counter. Two men, two pistols on two and a half feet of counter. I said to my friends, "I don't see a back door. Reckon where do you think they want one?" As the conversation heated up, a man gets up from one of the tables up front, walks up behind the angry customer and whacks him on the back of the head with a slapjack. Then he handcuffs him, takes him out to his unmarked car, puts him in the back seat, and comes back in and finishes his barbeque. Only at Harold's. Man, I miss that place.

Pigs Smell Better Cooked Bibliography

S. Jonathan Bass, *How 'bout a Hand for the Hog': The Enduring Nature of the Swine as a Cultural Symbol of the South,* Southern Culture, Vol. 1, No. 3, Spring 1995.

Craig Claiborne. *Southern Cooking.* New York: Times Books, 1987.

Mary Douglas, ed. *Food in the Social Order.* New York: Russell Sage Foundation, 1984.

John Egerton. *Southern Food: At Home, On the Road, In History.* New York: Alfred A Knopf, 1987.

Sam Bowers Hilliard. *Hog Meat and Hoecake: Food Supply in the Old South.* Carbondale: Southern Illinois University Press, 1972.

Jeremy MacClancy. *Consuming Culture: Why You Eat What You Eat.* New York: Henry Holt and Company, 1992.

James Donald Mackenzie. *Colorful Heritage: An Informal History of Barbeque Presbyterian Church and Bluff Presbyterian Church.* Olivia, NC: Rev. James Mackenzie, 1969.

Ernest Matthew Mickler. *White Trash Cooking.* Berkeley: 10 Speed Press, 1986.

Charles L. Perdue, Jr., ed. *Pigsfoot Jelly and Persimmon Beer.* Santa Fe: Ancient City Press, 1992.

Joe Gray Taylor. *Eating, Drinking and Visiting in the Old South.* Baton Rouge: Louisiana State University Press, 1982.

Mary Anne Schofield, ed. *Cooking by the Book: Food in Literature and Culture.* Bowling Green: Bowling Green State University Popular Press, 1989.

Jane and Michael Stern. *Good Food.* New York: Alfred A. Knopf,

1983.

Charles Reagan Wilson and William Ferris, eds. *Encyclopedia of Southern Culture*. Chapel Hill: UNC Press, 1989.

OLD FRIENDS

We move in different circles now
Elliptical and ever further apart
and yet when our courses do intersect
we discover we are still connected at the heart.

Past experiences shared galvanize us
Sealing and protecting our friendship from life's storms.
Sight is not necessary for communion
when constant presence in thought is the norm.

The incidents and accidents of living move us further on
toward the opening of that final door.
Passage will cause one of us pain,
but the other will know that none has loved him more.

A PEANUT BY ANY OTHER NAME IS STILL A LEGUME

I have a confession to make. It borders on blasphemy. I've sought forgiveness, and the Lord has been gracious to me. Here it is, I came to love boiled peanuts late. There, I've said it. I feel better already.

I will continue my catharsis. For years I considered boil' ground peas a slimy ruination of a Southern staple. I grew up in a parched peanut home. Are you familiar with the term "parched" used in relation to peanuts? Parched is the same thing as roasted. It was a joyous treat for my Dad, Morris Freeman. When the raw peanuts arrived at Brannan's Store around October first dad would buy a 10-pound sack. He'd cover a large-sided baking sheet with the lovely legume. Then he put them in a cold oven. Next, he set the oven temperature to 400 degrees. When the oven temperature hit 400 degrees, he turned it off. Dad left the peanuts in the oven until the pan cooled enough to take out bare handed. He always said "Ha-Cha" as he poured the nuts into a large bowl. Smiling happily, we'd dive in.

Now, back to boil' peanuts. Yes, it's boil' peanuts. The "-ed" is silent. Y'all knew that, right. I've already admitted that that I came to boil' peanuts late. They don't look too tasty. And the shells, what do you do with the shells? You can spit an olive pit unnoticed into a napkin. There's no discreet way to dispose of a wet peanut shell.

Friends, the only way to eat boil' goober peas is straight from the container. Be it plastic bag or Styrofoam cup. If they're in a paper bag, something's awry. I'd question the integrity of the seller if they tried to hand me a poke of boil' peanuts. The best way to eat boil' peanuts is going eighty down 85. That's 80 miles an hour on Interstate 85. Backroads require slower speeds, but the same principles apply. You steer with your wrists. Why? Because your hands are slick and sticky from the saltwater running down your fingers. Just put the container in the cup holder. Reach over and grab a nut and pop it in your mouth. With practice you'll be able to crack the peanut with your teeth and extract the lovely meat with your tongue. At that point it's acceptable to spit the hull out the window. Some, more delicate folks spit the hull into their hand and toss it out the window. To each his own. You can justify this because they're biodegradable. And they turn into mulch a lot faster than apple cores. Well, let's face it: They're close to mulch when you eat them. When eating boil' peanuts inside it's best done at the sink. You'll need a trash can next to you for the hulls. If you're lucky your sink will have a high-power disposal. If so, drop the shells in the drain and flip the switch. The disposal method makes it impossible for anyone to know how many you can consume in one sitting.

I pull over when I see hand-lettered BOIL P-NUTS signs. In the fall, in the South they're everywhere, and then they're not. The problem with boil' goobers is sourcing. Let's say a boil' peanuts sign appears at a four-way stop. Great, but it may, or may not be there the next time. Sellers are apparently ignorant of the law of supply-and-demand. I'm demanding them, and I can't find a supply.

My favorite source was at the four-way stop (now a round-about) in Bold Springs Georgia. The proprietor was a skinny, grizzled fellow. He always wore shorts. His shins were covered in tattoos of dragons. The gentleman was old school. He boiled his product in a cast iron cauldron over a wood fire. No sir, no propane for him. He dipped the peanuts by dragging a flat, pierced ladle the size of a colander through the soupy water. That water was the color of Marbury Creek Swamp outside Winder, Georgia. I speed up when I go through a swamp. Swamp things dwell in my worst nightmares. Anyway, steam rose off the water. The thing looked like a prop from a Halloween haunted house. The irregular shapes of the peanuts floated on top like pale larvae. "Food for the gods," I tell tattoo-man. He says, "Yep, my son is in Afghanistan, and when he comes home, the first thing he wants is boil' peanuts." I cried all the way home thinking about that boy.

The scarcity of a consistent source leads to desperate measures. Having a craving flung on me, I searched out the local farmer's markets, and fruit and vegetable stands. The only boil' peanuts I could find were just outside Monroe, Georgia. As the lady dipped my peanuts, I asked why they were getting so hard to find. "Folks can't get a permit," she said. Ah. That explained the here-today-gone-tomorrow aspect. Dodging John Law, or the health inspector, I guess. Did you make these? I asked. She gave me the stink eye, and answered, "Yes." I didn't stay and look for a permit.

I even stooped so low as to put out a Facebook SOS. The responses weren't very satisfying: "Want me to bring you some from Athens?" "You can get raw ones at the Dekalb Farmer's Market." "I believe someone was boiling them in Loganville last week ..."

On to the Georgia Department of Agriculture website. There I found color-coded charts of vegetables seasonally available at farmers markets. For a moment I was back in elementary school working on a word problem. It felt like this, "There's a group of 10 people who are ordering pizza. If each person gets 2 slices and each pizza has 4 slices, how many pizzas should they order?" Two products were represented with solid horizontal lines through spring, summer, fall, and winter: sweet potatoes and peanuts. All those peanuts, omnipresent as Forrest Gump's shrimp. Raw, dried, salted, roasted, mashed, fried. Peanut brittle, peanut butter. But what about boil'? Nothing.

As the old proverb says, necessity is the mother of invention. I'd have to solve the sourcing issue my own self if I wanted a stable supply of product. So, out came the big pot and the crock pot. Heck, I even thought about trying a neti pot. After procuring some bags of raw and green peanuts I went to work. What followed was a month of trial and error. I soaked the raw ones overnight and cooked on high in the crock pot for eight hours. I soaked the green ones overnight and boiled them for four hours. I didn't soak and boiled in water and Tony Chachere's Original Creole Seasoning. I didn't soak and boiled in vinegar. I measured the salt precisely. I randomly shook the saltshaker over the pot. And so on. A perfect boil' peanut is about texture. Getting the right amount of mush is critical and driven by preference. There's no such thing as al dente with boil' peanuts; no soft is too soft. Saltiness is also critical. Like a tomato sandwich is a vehicle for Blue Plate mayonnaise, a boil' peanut is a vehicle for salt. I stirred water that resembled the stuff passing as water in my birdbath. It was tiresome; I burned a lot of incense. I listened to untold hours of bluegrass music. It was brutal, but in the end…Eureka! I found the holy grail of boil' peanuts. So, listen up: Empty a bag of raw peanuts into a crock pot (aka slow cooker), cover with water, stir in a cup of salt, and cook on high for 24 hours. Works every time.

Whether you call them boiled, boil', "bald" or the Caviar of the South, boil' peanuts are addictive. Thank goodness I cracked the code, and now, dear reader, you have too. Add another punch to my Southerner card.

AUTUMN

The multi-colored leaves fall.
Tumbling and floating as they do.
Chilly winds blow, skipping them along the ground.
Autumn has arrived.

Little children run and jump into the piles of leaves.
Scattering those their father has raked with glee.
The clear blue sky is streaked with smoke as the leaves are burned.
The smell of Autumn fills the air.

Autumn always brings back memories of another place,
Another time.
The foolish actions of a young man so very long ago,
But nothing can be changed for
Autumn has arrived.

MOM'S CHOCOLATE PIE

Mom had two go-to pies. Coconut cream, and chocolate. Here's the recipe for the chocolate…

Ingredients

- 1 ½ cups sugar
- 2 cups whole milk
- ½ cup corn starch
- ½ cocoa
- Pinch of salt
- 3 eggs, separated
- 4 tablespoons salted butter
- 1 teaspoon vanilla

- 1 unbaked pie crust, store bought or homemade

Filling Instructions

1. Preheat the oven to 350 degrees Fahrenheit.

2. Make a homemade pie crust (like Mom) or use a store-bought pie crust. Roll it out and place it into a pie dish. Finish the edges however you like and bake until golden brown and set aside to cool.

3. Separate eggs, place yolks and eggs in separate bowls.

4. Using hand or stand mixer mix all ingredients except egg yolks.

5. Slowly beat egg yolks until fully mixed

6. Add beaten egg yolks to mixture. Mix until fully blended.

7. Cook pie filling in double boiler stirring until it thickens.

8. Pour thickened filling into cool pie shell.

Meringue Instructions

1. Beat egg whites until foamy.

2. Add pinch of Cream of Tartar and 6 tablespoons of sugar to foamy egg whites.

3. Beat until mixture peaks.

4. Spread meringue over chocolate filling.

Finish the Pie Instructions

1. Place in preheated oven (350 degrees Fahrenheit) until meringue browns.

2. Remove and set aside to cool.

SOUTHERN WORDS AND PHRASES, AND HOW WE USE THEM

I've written about the origins of our beautiful drawl in a previous chapter, *Southern, It's What I Am*. I think it wise, maybe educational for some of y'all, to expound on the nuances of how we use our native tongue. Many have attempted to convey this information. There are even dictionaries of Southern words. Tragically, most of these products are found in the novelty sections of stores like Buc-ee's and Cracker Barrel. In days-gone-by such books were carried by Spencer's Gifts and Stuckey's. Well, let's, "git er done."

Ok, stop right there. The last phrase in the paragraph above was never uttered by a Southerner until recently. It was created by a guy raised on a pig farm in Nebraska. A guy that went to high school in West Palm Beach, Florida, one of the ritziest coastal towns in America. His Southern accent ain't real. He describes himself as a 'linguist chameleon'. He's an actor. A classically trained actor. Dan Whitney (Larry the Cable Guy) has made a fortune at his craft. More power to him, but he ain't a Southerner. He plays one on TV.

Now, back to the real stuff. Do you know the difference between a hissy fit and a conniption fit? Typically, Southerners are known for our good manners. We say, "yes ma'am" and "no sir." It's as natural as breathing for us to invite strangers to sit a spell on our porch. We'll even offer them a glass of sweet tea (more about sweet tea later).

Sometimes we're not polite. No human being is always polite. Things happen that make us not-so-polite. Like when we go to a restaurant, and they don't serve sweet tea. Or someone serves stuffing instead of dressing at Thanksgiving dinner. Or when they make fun of our accents. When things like that happen, we have two choices of fit to pitch: a hissy fit, or a conniption fit. Notice I said "pitch" and not "have." You may be saying, "What are you talking about?" Well, here's some of that educating I promised.

Here's how the venerable *Oxford English Dictionary* defines a hissy fit: "n. chiefly U.S. a fit of temper, an angry outburst, a tantrum." Let me explain. A hissy fit is what happens in the toy aisle at Wal-Mart. It's what your kid does when you tell them they can't have a toy.

My favorite use of the term in pop culture is from Alabama native Fannie Flagg. She wrote in her book "*Daisy Fae and the Miracle Man,*" that "Momma always looks like she is on the verge of a hissy fit, but that's mainly because when she was eighteen, she stuck her head in a gas oven looking at some biscuits and blew her eyebrows off."

I must tell you friends, there's a fit worse than a hissy fit. What could be worse, you ask? A conniption fit. It too is pitched and not had. Conniptions are when a hissy fit becomes physical. For example, let's say you're in the throes of a hissy fit and start flinging your arms wildly. You, my friend, are pitching a conniption fit. What's the best thing to do when confronted with a conniption? Run. Run like your hair is on fire and the Boogie Man is chasing you.

Now you know, act accordingly.

How about "Rurnt " "Rurnt" is an altered form of the word

"ruined." Don't ask me how that second "r" came to be there. "Rurnt" is a made-up word. Why did Southerners make it up? Because it's just a better word. It has one syllable, while ruined has two. "Rurnt," when used in reference to a person, means they're spoiled or have wasted potential. "Rurnt" used in a sentence, "Her daddy just rurnt her with that new car when she turned 16." It's also used to describe something organic that's fading fast, as in, "That cabbage is rurnt." Or "Them leftovers is rurnt."

A Southerner knows exactly how many crappie (a fish), collard greens, turnip greens, peas, beans, yeller squash, okra, and so on, make up "a mess." "Mess" can also mean "disorganized, untidy or in an unpleasant condition," such as, "That boy's room is a mess."

In the South, "mess" is also a character trait. We say, "That girl is such a mess!" There's a problem when we use mess this way. The previous sentence has two meanings. It all depends on the voice inflection. Said with a smile and cheery tone, it means "That girl is cuter than a speckled puppy." Say it with a frown and a mean voice it means, "That girl's going to end up a streetwalker, y'all. Mark my words."

And "yonder,"as in "over yonder." Only a Southerner can show you the general direction of "yonder." Before we define "yonder," let's see how this wonderful Southern word is used in a sentence. When talking about a place, either near or some distance away, you might say:

"Where do your Mama 'em stay at?"

"They stay down yonder in Granny's old house-place by the peach orchard."

Or is used to show direction:

"We're lost as Hogan's goat. Whichaway, should we go?"

"I say we head over yonder way. I think I hear the road."

It's important to note that "yonder" is used with "down" or "over" or "up." It can be used to tell where a something is. You can say:

"You see that hawk? It's right yonder through them trees."

Or a little bit different, but the same:

"Where's my hoe? Why yonder it lays."

In yonder's vagueness lies one of its beauties. It's a great way to answer a question. Especially when you don't know the answer or don't want to say. Like this example:

"Where's Lucinda?"

"Well, I can't say, Bud. I think I saw her walk over yonder with Clem."

Yonder is accompanied by a point, nod, or glance. When we aren't sure, we gesture in the general direction of "yonder." That's about as accurate as we get. Another beauty of "yonder" is what I call its vague specificness.

A phrase like, "the goats eat, yonder" is just a way to say, "over there." "Over there" is 10 inches, 10 feet, or 10 miles away. It implies a distance that's not too great from where you are. There are exceptions of course. If you use "yonder" with "wild" and "blue" in the distance is great. Very, very great indeed.

Southerners know exactly how long "directly" is. As in the phrase: "Going to the store, be back directly." By the way, directly is pronounced "drectly".

Babies in the South come into this world knowing what "Gimme some sugar" means. It has nothing to do with the white, sweet stuff mama keeps in a little bowl on the table. It means give me a kiss. It's acceptable to replace "me" with your relation to the person (such as mama, granny, aunt). It'd sound like this: "Come over here and give yo mama some sugar."

Or the more general, "Oh, it's been too long, darling, give me some sugar!" It's perfectly fine to answer the request with the question: "Granulated or smack-u-lated?"

We know exactly when "by and by" is. Our great hope is that it will be sweet. Like the old hymn says, "In the sweet by and by, when we meet on that beautify shore." We don't use the term much anymore, but we know the concept very well.

Instinct dictates to the Southerner how to comfort a neighbor. They can be losing a loved one, going through a bankruptcy, or a divorce, it doesn't really matter. A plate of fried chicken and some cold potato salad is the answer. If the neighbor is in a real crisis, we add a large banana puddin!

Only Southerners know the difference between "right near" and "a right fer piece." They also know that "just down the road" can be 1 mile or 20. Also, no true Southerner ever believes the car with their blinker on is going to turn. Another inherent piece of Southern knowledge is about the word "fixin." "Fixin" is used as a noun, a verb, or an adverb. Also, we make friends standing in lines. When we're "in line," we talk to everybody.

Genealogy is a big deal in the South. The reason? If there're 100 Southerners in a room half of them are related, if only by marriage. The genealogy helps to figure out the connections. We share a lot of ancestors. For instance, my wife and I share a common ancestor, Thomas Camp III, 1717 – 1798. Thomas is her eighth-great-grandfather. He's my sixth-great-grandfather. Six degrees of separation, and all that.

Y'all is the most used word in the South. And according to the BBC its usage is beginning to migrate. They say in the past couple of years, "y'all" has exploded in use. Especially among people far outside the South. Y'all is showing up in places north of the Mason-Dixon Line in the US, like New York City, and even in many countries overseas. Just remember, you heard it here first. Also, in the South, "y'all" is singular, "all y'all" is plural.

Southerners know where grits come from (corn). We also know how to eat them. Grits are not a cereal, don't eat them like they are. No sugar in grits, period. I believe this is the unwritten eleventh commandment. It's OK to put cheese in grits. It must be sharp cheddar, or old-fashioned red-rind hoop cheese. Shrimp and grits together are alright.

Speaking of cheese grits. One time, years ago, a bunch of us guys went fishing at Lake Sinclair near Milledgeville, Georgia. A friend, Tony Baird, and his family owned a fishing cabin right on the water. One morning I had breakfast duty with Ken Carnegie. Ken was a South Georgia guy. He learned to cook grits from his grandmother. I'd cooked grits before, but they were always lumpy. As we fired up the stove Ken said, "I got the grits Freeman. You scramble the eggs." Fine with me because I could watch Ken's grits making exhibition. Never stop learning, I say. As he got started, I asked what his secret was. He replied, "Never stop stirring. From the time you pour em in the pot till you take em up. Never stop stirring." Then he added, "And Freeman, don't put the cheese in until right before you take em up. If you've done it right the grits will melt that cheese in a second. Your stirring will mix it good. That's what my granny taught me. That's what I've always done. Works every time." He was right. Those were the best grits I'd ever tasted. As I write this, I must pause a minute and reflect. Ken is no longer with us. Kidney disease took him several years ago. Another friend, Bill Adams, has also passed. Heart disease finally got him. And Steve "Boomer" Jones is gone too. Steve had COPD. I miss them all. God rest their souls. See y'all in the sweet by and by. Thanks for your indulgence, dear reader.

In the South, tomatoes are eaten at breakfast. Served with eggs, hog sausage, hog bacon, grits, and coffee they're wonderful. Red-eye gravy (look it up) is also a breakfast food.

Especially when served with cathead biscuits. Oh, and fried green tomatoes ain't a breakfast food.

I reckon you've heard "reckon" before. It can replace words like think, suppose, or assume. It can also be way to begrudgingly agree. For instance, "Honey, are you ready to go to my mamas for supper?" could be answered with a simple, "I reckon." But "Hell, I reckon" is different. The addition of "hell," plus a little exasperation, changes the phrase entirely.

Now, about sweet tea. True Southerners say, "sweet tea" and "sweet milk." Sweet tea is sweetened with white, Dixie Crystal sugar, and lots of it. Don't serve us tea unsweetened. That's the eighth deadly sin. "Sweet milk" means whole cow's milk. Not two percent, skim, lactose free, goat, sheep, yak, or any kind of nut or grain, so called "milk." If we say sweet milk, we don't want buttermilk. By the way, I had no idea that nuts and grains had teats. That makes them milkable, I guess. Who knew?

As a rule, a Southerner doesn't scream obscenities. That's unless there's a hammer and a body part involved, usually a thumb or fore finger. We don't cuss or gesture at little old ladies who drive 30 MPH in the left lane of the expressway. We just say," Bless her heart," and move right along.

"Bless your heart" is a great Southern phrase. It's widely used and, like other uniquely Southern phrases, it's versatile. Often, it's a declaration of true consolation. Like when something horrible happens and we're at a loss for words. Sometimes, "bless their/your/his/her heart" is all that's uttered. However, frequently, it's a statement of disapproval. Don't let it bother you though. Everyone down here has been on the receiving end of an exasperated "bless your heart." Some of us more than others. Modifiers are sometimes included. Things like "ever-lovin'," "pea-pickin'," or "little bitty." Those are just seasoning. The true difference between consolation and disapproval is in the tone.

This is not meant to be an exhaustive list. Southerners are creative with language. I cite William Faulkner, Robert Penn Warren, Eudora Welty, Winston Groom, and Elisabeth Donnelly as examples. Many of the words and phrases I've pointed out have many variations. I hope you learned something you didn't know.

For those who're still a little embarrassed by your Southerness: Take two tent revivals and a dose of sausage gravy and call me in the morning. Bless your heart!

And for those that ain't from the South. If you've lived here a long time. Get y'all a sign for y'alls front porch that says, "I ain't from the South, but I got here as fast as I could."

THOUGHTS AROUSED BY A GLANCE

I catch you out of the corner of my eye
and I take a quick, cautious glance at you.
Your brown skin causes me to tense up
with fear at first, and then anger at myself.

Why do I react this way when I see you?
What's within me that causes this reaction?
It makes me angry and sad that sometimes these
feelings still exist no matter how hard I try.

Do you feel the same way when you see me?
God knows you have more of a right than I
to have this primeval fear steal the very breath
from your throat and cause your heart to pound.

Deep in your minds darkest recesses the memories
of another place and another time must still reside.
Bullwhips crack and women and children cry because
their men have been torn away and sold, or worse.

I don't blame you for the way you must feel,
and I'm sorry for the pain it still causes you.
Help me to understand my feelings of fear,
or is it guilt for something I never did.
Do you know?

Somewhere the cycle of separation must be broken.
Somehow, we both must exorcise our demons
before they consume us or consume us, they will.
The demons of hatred and racism love us neither one.

We must then learn to love each other to survive.

MARCH 1963

I was 10 years old when I had my first experience with the dead. I knew about death in a cowboy kind of way. I'd seen many men die on *Gunsmoke*. *Gunsmoke* was a regular thing for Papa Freeman and me. We loved Festus. We wondered about Marshall Dillon and Miss Kitty. Well, Papa did, I was oblivious. Marshal Dillion was a deadeye with his Colt 45. He never lost a gunfight. Our other regular programs included *The Rebel*, *The Lone Ranger*, and *The Rifleman*. They all included dramatic deaths. No blood and guts like we see today, but when the Lone Ranger dropped them, they were graveyard dead. Papa liked Live Atlanta Wrestling, or as he called it, "Rasslin." No death there, but he sure thought it was real. I'd been to funerals. At least I'd been to one. My great grandfather, James William Campbell, died in 1958. I was six years old, so I didn't really understand what was going on.

I'll never forget early Sunday morning March 10, 1963. The phone rang a little after 2 a.m. We had one phone, in the hall in the center of the house. I slept on the couch in the den. Dad had to come through my room to answer the call. I was sound asleep when I heard my mama scream. I'd never heard anything like it before. It scared me so bad I was afraid to get up to see what was happening. I just knew it was bad. Dad came into the den in a little bit and sat down on the couch next to me. He put his arm around me and said, "Son, I've got some bad news. Your Daddy Bob has died. That's why your mama is so upset. We're going to Stone Mountain to be with Nanny Pat. You stay here with Papa and Granny. OK?" "Yes sir,"

I said, and laid back down. I heard what he said, but I couldn't understand. I wasn't sure that I wanted too. After a while I fell back asleep.

I awoke the next morning to a familiar smell, coffee and bacon frying. I stumbled into the kitchen. Papa was sitting at the table. Granny was at the stove. She'd heard me flush the commode, so she had my coffee ready. Back then I took mine 2/3 coffee, 1/3 milk, and three heaping teaspoons of sugar. Papa said, "You alright boy?" I said, "Yes sir, but I had a bad dream last night. I dreamed Daddy Bob died." I saw the tears start to well in Papa's eyes. He said, "Son, I'm so sorry. That was no dream. Daddy Bob is gone." I screamed, "No!" Then ran back to my room and fell sobbing onto the couch.

Dear reader, I think it's a good idea to tell you a little about Daddy Bob. I'm not sure words can do him justice, but I'll try. He was born Cylvester Robert Attaway. He came into this world on July 5, 1910. He was born at the family farm in the community of Bold Springs Georgia. Here's a picture of Daddy Bob and family in 1918.

He's the boy in the middle between his mom and dad. His parents were James Holman Attaway and Dora Lewis Biggers. He was the fifth child of ten. His young life was spent doing things farm boys do. Things like feeding the chickens, slopping the hogs, and helping with the plowing, planting, and picking the crops his daddy grew. By the age of 13 Daddy Bob was finished with school. This was typical for the time. Most rural students went just long enough to get basic math, reading, and English skills. He only had a seventh-grade education.

In the early 1920's the price of cotton dropped from 41 cents a pound to 13 cents a pound. Like most farmers of that era, Daddy Bob's father James began to struggle. He fought hard, but eventually lost the farm. It's a family legend that Grandmother Attaway never forgave James. She blamed him for losing the farm. By all accounts she was a hard woman. Sometimes life makes a person that way. By 1930 the family had moved to Stone Mountain Georgia. By March of that year Daddy Bob and Sarah Vertice Lunsford were married. Here's the happy couple.

He was working as a clerk at a rubber manufacturing company in Atlanta. They rented their home and didn't own a radio. I don't think they had time for one.

Daddy Bob and Vertice were busy during the thirties. They had five kids between 1931 and 1936. To be fair, there was a set of twins in the mix, my mother Vertice (Molly) and her sister LaVertice (Polly). In the mid-thirties Daddy Bob went to work at The Georgia Railway and Power Company. He drove a streetcar. Sadly, it was to be a short marriage. On New Year's Eve 1938 Vertice took sick. A head cold rapidly turned into a sinus infection. A sinus infection became pansinusitis. The pansinusitis migrated to her spine causing meningitis. Everything went septic, and septicemia set in. By the time they got her to Emory Hospital it was too late. She died on January 8, 1939. She was only 29. A widower with five small children. It's hard to imagine the grief and stress Daddy Bob felt, but somehow, he went on.

In 1941 a young woman got on his streetcar near the Atlanta YWCA. Her name was Martha Cleo Patterson. Martha, everyone called her Pat, was from rural Franklin County, Georgia. Like a lot of girls, she'd come to Atlanta looking for work. She found it at Fort McPherson. There was a war on, you know. Anyway, sparks flew, and they were married on December 20, 1942. That's how Nanny Pat came into the family.

I was born on October 23, 1952. It was a cold and stormy night, so I've been told. I was there, but I have no recollection. Here's my birth announcement as it appeared in the Atlanta Transit newsletter, *Two Bells*.

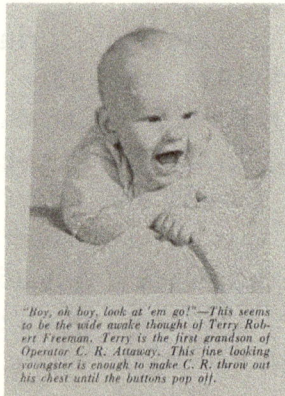

"Boy, oh boy, look at 'em go!"—This seems to be the wide awake thought of Terry Robert Freeman. Terry is the first grandson of Operator C. R. Attaway. This fine looking youngster is enough to make C. R. throw out his chest until the buttons pop off.

Two Bells was published from the 1930's until 1960's. It was started by the Georgia Power and Railway Company and survived the transition to the Atlanta Transit Company. I was Daddy Bob's first grandchild, so I was a big deal. A similar announcement was published in Georgia Power's monthly newsletter *The Citizen*. That was dad's workplace. I won't bore you with that one. I will say, I was one cute baby. I wonder what went wrong.

Daddy Bob was an integral part of my life for the first ten years. Other than Papa and Granny Freeman, who I saw every day, my earliest memories are of him. He'd come and get me and take me to work with him. By that time diesel buses had replaced the streetcars, and trackless trolleys. His route was a round-tripper from Stone Mountain to Atlanta. He'd sit me in the seat right behind him. I got introduced to everyone. I told you I was a big deal.

Mom often told a story about me and Daddy Bob. It goes like this. One Saturday he picked me up for work. She told him, "Daddy, don't buy that youngen' nothing. He's got more now than he can play with. You know if you stop, he's going to want something. Just don't do it." He said, "OK," and off we went. We stopped at the store just before we got to the bus barn. He always got come cigars for the day. I was looking around and I saw a little, red fire truck. I took it to Daddy Bob, and he bought it for me. Of course, he did. At the end of our workday, we arrived back home. I jumped out of the car and ran to show Mom my new toy. Daddy Bob was right behind me. Mom saw my fire truck and began to scold him. "Daddy, I told you he would want something, and I told you not to buy him anything!," she said. His response was classic Daddy Bob. He said, "Honey, he didn't say he wanted a thing." She said, "Well what's that?" pointing at my little red fire truck. He said, "Oh that, he didn't say he 'wanted' it. He brought it to me and said he 'needed' it." What could she say? I "needed" it.

Now back to that time in early March 1963. Nanny Pat's birthday was March 9th. Daddy Bob took her out to eat. They got home about ten-thirty and went straight to bed. Around twelve-thirty Sunday morning she heard a loud thud. She jumped out of bed to find Daddy Bob face down on the bathroom floor. She immediately called Dr. McCurdy who came right over. There was nothing he could do. When he called dad at 2 A.M. he told him that Daddy Bob had a massive heart attack. The one they call the widow maker. Dr. McCurdy said he was dead before he hit the floor. Thus, began my introduction to death in its rawest form. At least it was for me.

Monday afternoon Mom and Dad took Papa, Granny, and me to see Daddy Bob. Dad drove to the little brick house on Sagewood Circle. There were a lot of cars. We went up the steps to the stoop, and on into the living room. Nanny Pat came to me, and we both started to cry. After we had a good cry she said, "Do you want to see Daddy Bob?" I wasn't sure if I did or not. I thought he was dead. I was confused as we made our way across the room to the casket. And there he was. Asleep, or so my 10-year-old mind thought. Sure, he's asleep. I can see him breathing. I was more confused than ever. I pulled away from Nanny Pat and ran out to pet the beagles. Daddy Bob was a rabbit hunter. He had five or six beagles in a pen in the back yard. I spent the rest of the day with them. Even as we were leaving, I never looked at Daddy Bob again. I said not a word on the drive home.

I'll pause here to look at why we found Daddy Bob in a casket in the living room. Years ago, it was customary to bring a deceased loved one home. For the old timers it was called "laying a corpse." As in, "Mr. Johnson is laying a corpse at his mama's house." It's sometimes called "settin' with the dead." You might hear, "Me and Lew are settin' with the dead for Mr. Sawyer." Both can be done at home or at a funeral home. Nowadays, it's mostly at funeral homes, if done at all.

The origin of the custom of "settin' with the dead" is lost to the mists of time. Some say it's a Celtic tradition and came with the Scotch-Irish to America. No one really knows. Before embalming and funeral homes, a handmade quilt was placed over the body. Underneath the quilt a layer of herbs and spices were sprinkled. On top of the quilt, they'd put more herbs and spices, and then flowers. Sending flowers to a funeral came from this tradition. Remember, this was before embalming and fancy, air-conditioned funeral homes. The smell of herbs, spices, and flowers served a purpose. Here in the South, they helped hide the odor of decomposition. That's another reason why burial was one, no more than two, days after death.

I stayed home with Papa and Granny when Mom and Dad went back Tuesday. I knew the funeral was coming. I needed some time to get ready.

Wednesday morning, March 12th it was cold and raining. The clouds hung low, and pewter gray. The funeral was at 2:30 p.m. at First Baptist Church of Stone Mountain. His burial followed at Melwood Cemetery. The Masons of Stone Mountain Masonic Lodge Number 449, F&AM (Free and Accepted Masons) oversaw the graveside ceremony.

First the funeral. We sat in the car at the church waiting for Mr. Couch the undertaker to bring Daddy Bob. When the hearse arrived, the pallbearers got him out. We all fell in behind them as they carried Daddy Bob into the church. It was raining buckets. The umbrellas the adults carried were useless. Me, I took it like a man, albeit a wet one. The church was packed. The service was a blur. I think I was in shock. I do remember one song, *Beyond the Sunset*. The song was one of Daddy Bob's favorites. It was written in 1938 by Virgil Brock and his wife Blanche. They were Quakers, and then Mr. Brock became an evangelist in the Christian Church. He wrote the lyrics. Blanche wrote the music. Here's the second verse. That's the one that got me:

"Beyond the sunset, no clouds will gather,
No storms will threaten, no fears annoy.
O day of gladness, O Day unending,
Beyond the sunset eternal joy!"

Till this day, when I go into a church for the first time, I search their hymnal for *Beyond the Sunset*. If it's there, they're alright with me.

On to the cemetery. We all got soaked again going from the church to the car. It was about forty-five degrees, and the rain was relentless. We didn't fare much better at the graveside. My teeth were chattering as we made our way under the tent. It was dry there. The Masons performed their solemn ritual. I don't remember much except the fancy, lambskin aprons and the swords. I knew one of the men, Mr. Colbert Brannan. Mr. Brannan owned the store in Centerville where we traded. He was soaked too. The water was running down his face. Then I looked closer. He was crying. He and Daddy Bob were close friends. Like me, he was devastated by losing him.

As is the Southern tradition, we returned to Nanny Pat's house for the post burial meal. The ladies of First Baptist had cleaned the house. They reset the furniture in the living room and covered the dining room table with enough food to feed Sherman's army. After being so cold and wet it was nice to be in a warm house. Mom brought us a change of clothes too, God Bless her. I don't remember much about the food except it was good and plentiful.

After we said our goodbyes, we headed for home. I fell asleep and dreamed of Daddy Bob and his beagle hounds. I woke when Daddy picked me up to carry me inside. The hard rain had turned into a light drizzle. I was sad. Yes, about the last three days and the funeral, but there was something else. I couldn't stop thinking about the rabbit hunts that Daddy Bob and I would never have. Sixty years on I still miss him.

DADDY BOB

My Grandfather wouldn't drive a "City Slicker."
He said it was too big.
The old trolley bus suited him just fine.
He thought that "new bus" was too modern a rig.

He drove the Stone Mountain to Atlanta route
when I was just a kid.
Once and a while he'd let me come along.
It was the neatest thing I ever did.

His bus was small by today's standards.
No, it wasn't very big at all.
When I watched Daddy Bob wrestle the steering wheel
I felt I was ten feet tall.

All his passengers knew my name,
and that made me feel so good.
Daddy Bob bragged about me to everyone
just like I knew he would.

You see I was his little "Beetle Bum."
His very first grandchild.
I've been told that the day I was born
that he nearly went "hog-wild."

He died when I was ten years old.
That was over sixty years ago,
and I still miss him every day.
Oh, how I loved him so.

When I have passed from this blessed life,

having laid down the tools of this earthly job,
I hope my grandchild thinks of me
like I think of Daddy Bob.

MOM'S EASY PEACH COBBLER

Ain't many things better than peach cobbler. Especially right out of the oven with a slab of vanilla ice cream on top. Hush yo mouth! This one's so easy even I can make it.

Ingredients

- 1 cup white sugar
- ½ cup butter, room temperature
- 1 cup self-rising flour
- 1 cup milk
- 1 (15 ounce) can sliced peaches, with juice

Instructions

1. Preheat oven to 350 degrees.
2. Blend all ingredients. Use a blender, or a hand or stand mixer.
3. Place the peaches in the bottom of a 9x12 baking dish.

4. Pour the crust mixture over the peaches.
5. Place in oven, and bake for 30 to 45 minutes, until brown and bubbly.

Serve immediately with a big slab of vanilla ice cream.

GEORGIA RULES FOR LIVING AND SOME "POP-O-LOSOPHY"

Some rules are made to be broken. Then're are the rules we learn growing up in Georgia. These are rules that you break at your own peril. Georgia rules come in three different types: literal, open to interpretation, and specific. Here's an example of each. Literal, as in, turn off the light when you leave a room. Open to interpretation, if you can't do it right, don't do it at all. Here's an oddly specific one, never put tomatoes in a fruit salad. Parents have rules that kids are expected, nay required, to follow. Coupled with general rules for living, that's a lot of rules, y'all. And most, but not all, are worth following. I've numbered the rules, but only for clarity. They are in no meaningful order.

Here's one my mother lived by...

1. Don't Wear White Shoes After Labor Day, Or Before Easter.

You read that right friends, absolutely no white shoes after Labor Day or before Easter. Not only my mother, but all the women in my young life were religious about this rule. I almost broke this one once. I remember it well. It was the second Sunday in September. Dad had just bought me a pair of white Converse All-Stars. He found those beauties at Belk-Gallant's end-of-season sale. I couldn't wait to show them off. I got up Sunday morning, got dressed, and slipped them on. They looked great. Especially with my black pants, red shirt, and black skinny tie. Pleased with myself, I headed toward the kitchen for my morning coffee. Then it hit me. My shoes were white. Brand new too, so they almost glowed. I stopped in my tracks and headed back to my room. I needed a think. The fear of my mother and granny slapped me back into reality. I'd danced on the edge of the precipice. Thank God I didn't continue over the edge. I was a little queasy. I slipped out of my Converse and into my black loafers. Heck, I even took off my white socks and put on some black ones. Faux pas averted, I put my new shoes back in the box and into the closet. Man, won't they look sharp Easter.

Here's another important rule to live by...

2. Mind Your Manners.

This one might need some amplification. It's about respect. Especially respect for your elders. I was taught to respect my elders. It's something I still do. Even at the ripe young age of seventy. I toss respect at the young folks too. In hopes they'll learn to be respectful. Respect is simple. It starts with "yes ma'am," "no sir," "please," and "thank you". Holding a door for someone shows respect. How about, if you borrow something return it in a timely fashion. Also, take it back clean and in good working order. If you break it fix it or get them a new one.

This rule may be unique to my family...

3. Always Have Extra Presents Under The Tree At Christmas.

It's Christmas Day and company's coming. The usual suspects are expected, family and some friends. But what if someone brings a guest? An unexpected guest. What are you going to do? Not to worry at my house. We always have "guest" presents wrapped and under the tree. We used specific wrapping paper for male and female gifts to take out the guess work. Also, make sure the gifts don't have an expiration date. You can use them next year if you don't unexpected guests.

Here's a good one…

4. When There's Guests The Family Holds Back When Loading Their Plates.

When having guests, no matter the meal, the family holds back. This means we take the least desirable meats and small portions. You want the guests get plenty. I was 40-years old before I realized Granny Freeman practiced this rule. I was gob smacked to learn she like the breast. All I ever saw her eat was a wing or back of the fried chicken. So, this rule applies at family meals too. Granny's sacrifice made a white-meat only man out of me. God bless her.

This applies across the board. However, I think it was a man-only rule when first created.

5. Give A Firm Handshake.

My dad believed in a firm handshake. This, coupled with looking people in the eye makes a good impression. It also shows a person that you value meeting them and appreciate their time. A firm handshake is a sign of confidence.

We've learned the importance of respect with the mind your manners rule. This rule takes that one up a notch.

6. Always Show Respect For Your Elders.

Never refer to any adult by first name. Mr., Mrs., and Miss, followed by surname is the rule. Relatives are addressed by given name. If you place the relationship before it. For instance, Aunt Lucy, Uncle Howard, and so on. Always include the relationship. The rule is not age dependent. It applies no matter how old you are, or think you are. I still have scars from ignoring of this rule. It was my mother's eightieth birthday party. I was helping deliver slices of birthday cake. There was a table of uncles. I asked "Tink" (a nickname) if he wanted ice cream with his cake. My mother was standing close by and heard my question. She whipped her head around and gave me the stink eye. Uncle Tink looked disappointed. I quickly repeated the question, "Uncle Tink, would you like some ice cream with your cake?' Listen, my family ain't that big, but I must have been chastised by 100 people. Relatives and nonrelatives alike. Everyone reminded me it was Uncle Tink! Some even punched me on the arm as they delivered the rebuke. Lesson relearned.

Let's take a break from the rules for a moment. How about some "Pop-o-losophy." What is "Pop-o-losophy?" "Pop-o-losophy" is things my dad said to make a point. I doubt these thoughts were original to him, but he had a bunch of them. For instance...

"The Water Ain't Going To Clear Up Until You Get The Hogs Out Of The Branch."

I'd hear this one often. Usually when I was frustrated by people causing trouble. The meaning? The water of life will stay dirty until the troublemakers are gone. In fact, it's better to find another branch. So, don't hang out with troublemakers. If you find yourself surrounded by them, get away as fast as you can. No one should have to drink dirty water, so don't.

Or this one...

"...Crapping Green Squealing Worms."

When dad saw someone pitching a hissy fit, he'd use this one. Basically, he's saying they're overreacting. It works for conniption fits too. See the chapter *Southern Words and Phrases, and How We Use Them* to get a full description of these fits. I've also heard it a time or two in relation to fear. Maybe like this, "Jack was so scared when he stepped on that Copperhead, he was crapping green squealing worms!" I wonder what the heck green squealing worms are.

Now some more rules.

Here's two that go together.

7. Keep A Pair Of Good, Clean Pajamas Handy. Never Leave The House Without Wearing Clean Drawers.

Keep a pair of good, preferably new, pajamas handy. Just in case you must go to the hospital. I poo-pooed this idea in my younger years. But as I grew older, and the parent-child relationship reversed, I came to appreciate the logic. My wife and I spent six years caregiving for my parents. The rule didn't apply to Dad. He slept in his drawers. My mother, however, was a gown or pajamas gal. After she passed, I can't tell you how many brand-new pajamas we found in her bedroom. God rest her sweet soul. The other rule, the one about clean drawers, doesn't really matter. We still follow it though. Just in case you're in a wreck. I'm reminded of a story the late Southern humorist, Lewis Grizzard, told. Mr. Grizzard (did you catch that?) said his mama always asked him if his drawers was clean when he left the house. He always told her they were. Lewis said, "As I got in the car, I imagined this scenario. On my way to the Dairy Queen, I got hit by a semi-truck hauling hogs. They rushed me to the hospital. I'm in the ER, on a gurney, bleeding from every portal of my body. Two doctors are standing over me. One says, 'Good Lord ain't he a mess?' The other one replies, 'Yes, he is, but ain't his drawers clean? He must have a good mama.' Folks, I got news for you. If I get runover by a semi-truck hauling hogs, my drawers ain't gonna be clean. That's for sure!" Lewis was a hoot. He died of heart disease in 1994. In my opinion he was the Mark Twain of the 20th century. Oh, by the way, the truth is they cut off your clothes if you're in bad wreck. This is before you get to the ER.

I don't know why this a rule. Who would even consider such a thing?

8. Don't Poot At The Table.

I learned the consequences of breaking this rule as a little shaver. We were eating lunch, and I reached across the table for a biscuit. The strain was too much. I pooted. To be fair, I'd never heard of this rule. For little boys pooting is as natural as breathing. Anyway, Granny Freeman reached across the table and popped me on the head. Not one time, but twice. She said, "Boy don't never do that at the table." This rule apparently has a sub-rule. Never laugh when someone poots at the table. Papa Freeman I'm sure knew both rules. But he snickered when Granny popped me. She whirled in her chair and popped him twice too. Papa and me looked at each other. When Granny turned back to her plate Papa winked at me. I almost swallowed my tongue, but I didn't laugh.

This next one is self-evident.

9. Turn Off The Lights When You Leave A Room!

Yes, always turn off the lights when you leave a room! Or as we say in the South, "cut" off the lights. The rule is voided if someone's still in the room. That is unless you want to mess with them, or they're blind.

How about this one...

10. Never Pass Up A Chance To Tinkle.

This increases in importance with age. The older I get the more I follow this rule. That reminds me of a story. Some friends of mine, who shall remain nameless, reaped the consequences of ignoring it. They'd been down on the Georgia coast for a few days and were driving home. Coming northwest on US highway 341 you pass through Jesup, Georgia. After that, nothing for thirty miles or so. This unnamed husband and wife chose not to tinkle in Jesup. Even though they were both drinking Diet Cokes. This stretch of road is nothing but pine barrens and swamp. Occasionally, a sandy road cuts through the pines and weaves around the swamp. About ten miles out of Jessup the urge stuck him. He told his wife, "Baby, I gotta pee. I hope I can make it to Baxley." A couple of minutes later the urge got worse. My friend started to look for somewhere, anywhere, to go. He was almost passed it when he saw it. A little sandy road ran off into the woods to the right. He hit the brakes and turned in. Driving just far enough to not be seen from the main road, he stopped and jumped out. He left the door open. He began the deed. We've all been there. In an instant pain was replaced by the euphoria of relief. Then... He heard it before he saw it. The unmistakable sound of a diesel engine. Then the front of a yellow Wayne County school bus appeared. By this time, he was in full stream. No way to stop the flow. The bus was bearing down on him. His wife dropped to the floorboard and made herself as small as possible. During the maneuver, she started to howl with laughter. The poor guy was in a panic. What to do, then the faces of the kids started to appear in the windows. He clenched the offender with all his might and jumped into the car. The bus was passing. The flood continued unabated. It squirted through the steering wheel and splashed onto the windshield. The kids on the bus were laughing and pointing. The driver even tooted the horn. And just as quickly as it started it was over. The bus was gone. He got out of the car. The flood was now a trickle. There was a mess to clean up, and a wife to help get off the floorboard. She never stopped laughing. The moral of this tale. Well, there's two. Never pass a bathroom, and you ain't never as alone as you think you are.

This one is important. Well, they all are. This one may be importanter...

11. Keep Your Promises.

Try not to make promises. But if you make a promise, keep your promise. Another way of saying it is a promise made is a promise kept. As the old saying goes, your word is your bond. In a world where words are becoming meaningless make your words count.

Modern sensibilities suggest that this rule no longer applies. I beg to differ.

12. Don't Call Anyone After 9 P. M.

If you call me after 9 o'clock in the evening, you better be in the hospital. Or either your house or your hair is on fire. On second thought, don't call me that late unless your house is burning down. Your hair will grow back.

It takes a lot to make me mad. Violators of this rule make me pig biting mad.

13. Pay Your Respects For A Funeral Procession.

There ain't no excuse. Always, and I mean always, pull over to the side of the road and stop for a funeral procession. It's a sign of respect. Folks don't always seem to get that these days. One time I'd pulled over and stopped for a passing hearse. It was a long procession. I happened to look over to my right, and what I saw made me cry. A young man was weed whacking. When he saw the hearse, he stopped. He put down the machine. Then he stood up, took off his cap, and placed it over his heart, and bowed his head. He was raised right.

This probably ain't a rule, but it should be.

14. Don't Put Your Feet On The Furniture, Or The Dashboard.

Putting your feet on someone's furniture is not cool. It screams loudly that you don't respect them. I had a friend who'd put his shoe clad feet on the dashboard of my truck. Scratched it every time too. He even did it once with golf shoes on. I don't see the self-centered, pompous twit much anymore. Do you blame me?

An obvious rule if you know your plants.

16. Never Put Tomatoes In A Fruit Salad.

It's right up there with no shorts in church. It also means something else. A wise person always treats a janitor or a CEO the same. Treat them both with respect, and always be kind. By the way, a tomato is a fruit, but it doesn't go in a fruit salad. You're welcome.

How about some more "Pop-o-losophy?"

"Want In One Hand And Crap In The Other One. See Which One Gets Full The Fastest."

You don't always get what you want. Be thankful for what you have. I heard this one when I said I wanted something I didn't really need.

"If A Frog Had Wings, He Wouldn't Bump His Butt When He Hopped."

If this, if that, if I'd only. Dad used this one when I made excuses. Another version is, "If 'ifs' and 'buts' were candy and nuts it'd be Christmas every day."

"Well, I Swanny!"

We all knew he'd heard or seen something unbelievable. He also used it to mean I swear, or I promise. Like this, "Mort, didn't I tell you Goldwater couldn't win the election?' 'Yes, you did, I swanny'."

This is the last rule, and the most important.

17. Don't Just Say The Words, Show The Ones You Love How Much You Love 'Em.

My mom and dad told me, "I may not always love what you do, but I will always love you." We've told our son the same thing. The operative word in the rule is 'show'. Love is more than just three words. Love can be seen every day. It's shown by the man walking his beloved dog. You see it in the young man helping his neighbor carry her groceries. Sure, love is expressed in words, but I think more clearly by actions. Lester Bearden, one of the wisest men I've ever known said it like this, "I can't hear what you're saying because what you're doing is talking so loud," Even the smallest of gestures show love. Here's some actionable ideas. Give them a hug. In fact, the more hugs the better. Write them a letter and mail it to them. Shut your big yap and listen to them. If you can cook, cook them a meal. Spend some real quality time with them. Just show them.

JUDY'S "SPECIAL" MAC & CHEESE CASSEROLE

I love this. I can make a meal off it. It is so good.

Ingredients

- 8-ounce package of small macaroni shells, cooked
- 1-pound sharp cheddar cheese, grated
- 1 cup mayonnaise (Blue Plate of course)
- 4-ounce jar of pimento, chopped
- ½ medium onion, chopped
- 1 medium can of mushroom stems and pieces, chopped
- 1 can cream of mushroom soup
- 1 can water chestnuts, chopped
- 2 sleeves Ritz crackers, crushed
- 1 to 1 ½ sticks unsalted butter, melted

Instructions

1. Preheat oven to 325 degrees.
2. Combine all ingredients, except Ritz crackers and butter, in casserole dish. Mix well.
3. Melt butter.
4. Combine Ritz crackers with melted better in separate bowl. Sprinkle mixture on top of ingredients in casserole dish.
5. Bake for 40 – 45 minutes.

Enjoy!

FOR JUDY

Once I was alone.
I had few friends to laugh with me, to cry with me,
or to share my dreams.
Then I met you
and my life turned from a joke
into something real.

The wonderment of it all numbs my mind
and thrills me to the bone.
What was once ugly and empty
is now beautiful and full of life.

The broad awakening that someone
could really change my life.
I'm happy.

HOG KILLING TIME

Dear reader, this chapter is not for you if you're squeamish. I give the details, as best I can remember them, of killing and processing a hog. At times those memories are graphic. You've been warned. Note; if you choose to read on, I use the word hog and pig interchangeably.

I have memories of hog killing time. I shall attempt, in the next few paragraphs, to recount those memories. Memories are just that, memories. I'll do the best I can.

I witnessed hog killings as a young boy on the farm. Yes y'all, I grew up on a farm. Our little community of Centerville (the one in Gwinnett County, not Houston County) was rural. As was most of Gwinnett County from its founding in 1818 until the late 1960's. The nearest "big" town at that time was Lawrenceville. It's 12 miles to Lawrenceville, the county seat. The nearest town to the farm was Stone Mountain. It's 8 miles to Stone Mountain, and it's in another county.

A factoid: Georgia has 159 counties. Why so many? The Georgia State Constitution, that's why. At some point in the state's history, it included a provision about the location of county seats. It said that a county seat could be no more than a day's horseback ride from any citizen. That's why there are 159 counties, and not 50. Never stop learning y'all.

For years, cotton was the main cash crop in the county. It was harvested once a year, thus money was tight most of the time. Papa Freeman raised cotton, and some wheat. Everything else he grew was food. Winter was tough. Unlike today, November and December were cold months. That made those months hog killing time.

It took preparation to get a pig ready for slaughter. Hogs were usually fed food scraps, also known as slop. They'd pin up the pig or pigs destined for the table around the 1st of September. The fattening hogs still got slop, but also corn, lots of corn. Other than chicken, and a squirrel or rabbit now and then, pork was the family's meat. My Dad told me he'd never eaten beef until he went into the Air Force in 1951.

Hog killing was a yearly ritual. Like I said, very cold weather was needed to keep the meat from spoiling during processing. Here's how I remember a hog killing. Early in the morning, before daylight, the family and some neighbors would gather at the farm. The first thing they did was build a fire. It was built under a big cauldron for boiling water. When the water reached a rolling boil, it was ready.

Hog on a tri-pod

Then it was time to kill and bleed the hog. Hogs are killed in different ways. Papa preferred a .22 short round between-the-eyes. As soon as the animal was down it was hung on a tripod, and its throat slit. This sounds gross to our modern ears. I'm sure many folks today think their meat comes from a grocery store. But bleeding is critical. The meat won't keep without bleeding. Not bleeding also makes the meat taste "off". Some call this taste coppery. Whatever you call it the meat is rurnt (see chapter *Southern Words and Phrases, and How We Use Them*). Above is a picture of a hog on a tripod. The one Papa had looked just like that, except his had wheels. Wheels made it easier to move the hog around, to the different steps of the process. With the fire roaring, the next step was scalding and scraping.

The hog was rolled over to the boiling water. Today experts say the ideal temperature for scalding is 155°F. As far as I know, Papa never checked the temperature. He just dunked them. Scalding serves two purposes, cleaning, and hair removal. There's an art to scalding. It's important to not let the hog touch the hot cauldron. You don't want the hog sticking to it. Papa dipped the beast in and out of the water. He'd leave the pig in the water for 30 seconds to a minute and raise him up. They'd tug on the hair and dip the pig again. This was repeated until the hair was easy to pull out. If the fire's right this took from 3 to 5 minutes. Scalding too long would set the hair and if that happened it was hard to get off. When the hair was loose, they'd raise the pig out of the water, roll it away from the cauldron, and start scraping. Also, papa kept a bucket handy. If the skin started to cool before they could scrap it, they poured hot water from the scalding pot on it to warm it up. I told you it was an art. You also can see why neighbors were invited. It takes a crew to kill and process a hog.

At about this point, Granny and the ladies appeared. They brought hot coffee, biscuits, butter, and jelly. Mama would help if the killing was done on a weekend. Otherwise, she was at work in Atlanta.

After the brief respite, processing began in earnest. The hog was cut open from the head to the tail. More bleeding happens here. The organs were removed and saved in pans. The small intestines became casings to stuff the sausage in to make links. The large intestines were used for "chitlins." Chitlins were cleaned inside and out, so they say. I've never eaten chitlins. I have a fear of finding a piece of corn in one. I know, right? Granny had several pots of hot water on the stove. They used that water to clean the other organs and to rinse the whole hog. After a good cleaning, the hog was laid out on a heavy-duty table ready to cut up.

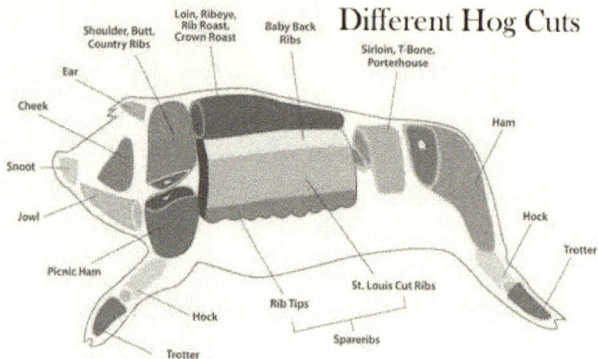

Different Hog Cuts

The hams and shoulders were removed first and trimmed of excess fat and bits of lean meat. They did the same with the feet. The head was cut off and laid aside. Next the tenderloin was removed. Traditionally, they ate the tenderloin that night for supper. Next came the middlings. Middlings are the meat between the shoulder and the ham and includes the spareribs, backbone, and fatback.

As the lean meat was trimmed, the women folk ground it for sausage. All the fat was saved to render for lard. Day one was about over. They placed the meat in the smoke house on tables to drain a bit more, and cure overnight. The head, heart, kidneys, liver, feet, ears, tongues, testicles (also known as mountain oysters), and other parts were shared with the neighbors that helped. Papa Freeman said, "We ate everything but the 'squeal.'" After a day's work like that no one had to be rocked to sleep that night.

On day two the hams and shoulders were rubbed with salt. Then they were placed in the salt boxes. The middlings and streak of lean were trimmed of fat and packed into the salt boxes. The salt boxes were in the smoke house.

Next it was time to mix and grind the sausage. Granny Freeman and the other ladies made the sausage. The ground sausage was mixed with red pepper flakes and other spices.

Then it was run again through the grinder again and stuffed into the casings (small intestines). This made very long pieces of link sausages. They kept out some of the sausage and fried it for lunch. They made a big batch of biscuits too. The links were hung from the ceiling of the smoke house. The large intestines were cleaned again, boiled, or fried as "chitlins". The hog head was boiled, and all meat removed for head cheese (see next paragraph). The brains were used too, scrambled with eggs.

Many of you, dear readers, may not be familiar with head cheese. Many folks think head cheese is a savory treat. Heck, Boar's Head even makes it today. Anyway, after several hours of boiling the bones and tissues release collagen. The collagen helps the finished head cheese solidify as it cools. Papa put salt, black pepper, and onion powder in his head cheese. Once the meat and fat have released from the skull the head was picked clean. They left a little fat on the meat and mixed the meat and spices by hand. The mixture was packed loaf pans. In earlier times it was packed into the pig's stomach. Head cheese was eaten quickly in the days before refrigeration.

They used the pig's feet to make pressed meat or souse meat. The feet were boiled, and the meat removed. Sometimes they were pickled. Granny fried the ears for lunch. Fried pig ear biscuits, anyone? The small pieces of fat were "rendered" (boiled) in a wash-pot. The lard was stored in old coffee cans, or Mason jars. During the rendering small pieces of lean meat and skin floated to the top. That stuff is called "cracklings". Ain't nothing better than a big, hot slice of cracklin' cornbread.

They boiled some of the fat with Red Devil Lye to make "Lye soap". When it cooled, they cut it into squares and chunks to use for washing clothes.

The salted meat was left in the salt box for a week to cure, and then wrapped hung in the smoke house.

Let's talk a little bit about the smoking process. Papa only used hardwood. He'd never use pine or other sappy woods. There're two reasons for that: 1. They give the meat a bitter flavor and 2. They make too much smoke. Oak was the smoking wood of choice although he used some hickory too. There was plenty oak on the farm. Papa paid close attention to the moisture in the wood. He'd never use freshly cut wood, it has too much water. And like the sappy woods it smokes too much and burns too slow. Seasoned wood is very low in moisture and burns better. The wood was cut into chunks. The smokehouse had a firebox. The fire should smolder. You want dense smoke, but not so thick you can't see through it. The hams, shoulders, and link sausage were hung so that they didn't touch. They smoked the meat until it turned chestnut brown. This took the hams and shoulders from 1 to 3 days, less for the sausage. Papa had to keep the fire constantly. If the weather was right and the meat was cured properly there was no spoilage. I'm telling y'all, it was an art, and labor intensive.

My brother-in-law, Clark Harrison, also grew up on a farm. By the way, he's written a memoir of his early years. The title is, *Farm Boy, Growing Up in the Forties and Fifties.* It's available on Amazon. Anyway, a few years ago, he decided he was going to kill a pig and process it. Friends, a hog has only 2 hams, and after the tenderloin, they're the most precious cut. As I've described, hog killing and processing is hard work. Clark salt cured his hams. I won't go into the methodology of salt curing. I will say that the ham is wrapped tightly in cheesecloth. A salt cured ham will often develop a green skim under the cheesecloth. It ain't spoiled, but if you don't know that, well stuff happens. Being the good Christian man he is,

Clark gave one of his hams to some friends at church. Time passed, and they hadn't mentioned the ham to him. More time passed, and Clark finally asked them how they liked the ham. They hemmed and hawed and finally said, "Clark, we hadn't said anything because we didn't want to embarrass you. It was spoiled. It was covered in this green stuff. So, we threw it away." Clark was flabbergasted. A perfectly good ham tossed out of ignorance. At least they could have asked.

As I remember, we always had hog meat to eat. Many times, it lasted until the next hog killing. Friends, you haven't lived until you've eaten a hot link sausage. Or a big slab of country ham soaking in "red eye" gravy. And don't forget the big "cat head" biscuit and mounds of scrambled cheesy eggs. My dad called this a "sawmill" breakfast. That's the breakfast you eat before going to work at sawmill!

I know all this is hard to believe, especially for you young folks but it's true; I remember it well, I think.

MOM'S NO-BAKE FRUITCAKE

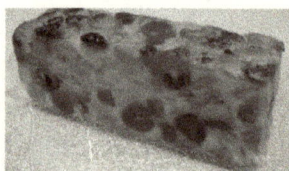

I know. A fruitcake recipe. Give this one a try if you don't like fruitcake. I didn't, until Mom started making this one.

Ingredients

- 3 sticks of salted butter
- 1 16-ounce package of marshmallows
- 1 13.5-ounce box of Graham Cracker crumbs
- 4 cups of coarsely chopped pecans
- ¼ cup brown sugar, firmly packed
- 2 teaspoons vanilla
- ½ pound candied mixed fruit, finely chopped
- ½ pound candied pineapple, chopped
- 2 8-ounce containers of candied red cherries
- 2 8-ounce containers of candied green cherries

Instructions

1. In top of a double boiler melt butter and marshmallows.

2. In a large bowl combine all other ingredients, mix well by hand.
3. Pour the melted butter and marshmallow mixture over the dry ingredients, mix well.
4. Shape into rolls, wrap in wax paper, place in refrigerator until cold.

Try it, you might like it!

THE CAMPFIRE REVELATION

I built a fire one evening.
We were camping and the night was cool.
It'd been a long time and I'd almost forgotten.
How could I have been such a fool?

The glow of the fire lit up our faces,
and the sparks floated off toward the stars.
The kids moved away, and we were left alone.
Your head on my shoulder began to heal the scars.

I'd been foolish and hurt, in many ways a child.
Harbored bitterness and I'm ashamed to say hate.
Knowing better doesn't always mean we do.
Once the healing starts you realize there's a better fate.

We snuggled under the blanket
closer than we'd been in a long, long time.
Not physically but spiritually we linked up again.
The road ahead may not be smooth, but it will be fine.

Life is a puzzle that has many missing parts.
We struggle to find them and sometimes lose our hearts.
The picture is still just as beautiful if we can only see
that it's the joy of working the puzzle together that sets us free.

I'VE BEEN TO THE PROMISED LAND

My daddy would say, "Let's go to the Promised Land," as we climbed into the car. For various reasons, we traveled down Highway 124 south from Centerville. Southeast Gwinnett County was rural back then. The crops we passed changed with the seasons. In late fall it was cotton, white and ready to pick. There were winter wheat fields, in the early spring, and some row crops in the summertime. 124 was a two-lane winding road. As we started down into the Yellow River valley the road went left. When you came out of the curve you entered a settlement of small comfortable homes. A little further down on the left, up on a hill, was a large two-story house. That house looked like it was from another era. It was, and it had a story to tell. That house was the "big house" of a former plantation called The Promised Land.

I'd like to tell The Promised Land's story opposite from the way it's usually told. Most often the account begins in 1820 with the arrival of a 17-year-old Irish immigrant in America. However, let's begin with an African American, Robert Livsey.

The Livsey family, both black and white, trace their family history to Rock Bridge in the antebellum era. Green Livsey, born in 1779, was the overseer on Robert Toombs plantation in Wilkes County. He moved to Gwinnett County in 1840 with his family of eight. While working on the Toombs Plantation, he had son, Sandy, with one of the female slaves. Sandy came with his father, there is no record of his mother coming. Maybe

Green brought her too, maybe he didn't. We don't know, and that's part of the tragedy that was slavery. By the 1870s, Sandy Livsey owned 138 acres in Harbins District. His half-brother, Green's son Charles H. Livsey, owned over 100 acres in the No Business Creek and Lee Road area. Thus, he was Thomas Maguire's neighbor on the northeast. Charles H. Livsey Jr. and F. I. Livsey later owned 64 acres of The Promised Land in the 1890s. Robert Livsey descended from Sandy Livsey. Robert and his wife Morena moved to southern Gwinnett County in the 1920s from the Dacula area.

We don't know exactly when they moved to the Big House. We do know from land records that he got the title deed in April 1926. The warranty deed was filed November 1, 1928. He paid cash, $2,500 he'd saved from his work with the railroad.

The early years at The Promised Land were challenging for the Livseys. The boll weevil had decimated cotton in the South. Then the Great Depression crippled the country. Livsey family oral history recalls the worry about possibly losing their land. Mr. Livsey used planned cultivation to keep his farm afloat while others around him were failing. He bartered with smoked hams and other farm foods to pay taxes. Taking care of family and providing for the community were important. Robert and Morena worked hard. They diversified the farm and had close relationships with their neighbors. All these things helped them to keep the farm and live comfortably. The Promised Land produced everything they needed to survive and thrive.

More about the farm...The Livseys slaughtered 4 to 5 hogs each year. Morena grew peanuts and sold them to make their tithe to New Bethel Church. The farm produced a variety of garden vegetables. Crops like potatoes, sweet potatoes, collard greens, cabbages, turnips, and carrots, which Morena canned for the winter. The fruit on the farm included apples, pears, plums, strawberries, watermelons, muscadines and scuppernongs, and blackberries. They also grew their own wheat and ground it into flour, and their mule-driven syrup mill made sorghum syrup. Robert took most meats, vegetables, and syrups to downtown Atlanta to sell at the farmer's market on Edgewood Avenue, later called the Sweet Auburn Market. I asked Thomas Livsey, Robert's son, what life was like on the farm. He laughed and said, "We didn't have Christmas every day, we went to the fields and worked."

Robert turned the pine wood into charcoal in earth pits. He sold these for people to use in coal iron presses when ironing clothes. Oak, and other hardwoods on the property was burned for heat in the wintertime. When crops produced poorly or weren't good enough to sell, he cut and sold firewood. From straw and thick fabric, Morena fashioned ticks for the family's bedding. Like Maguire before him, Mr. Livsey weaved cotton baskets to hold picked cotton. They were thrifty. Like most families they reused fertilizer and flour sacks to make clothes. They didn't waste anything and made good use of everything, like saving fruit peelings to make jelly.

Many things the Livseys did on the farm were typical farm practices. However, there were aspects of African American heritage at The Promised Land too. For instance, the yard as an extension of the house. Many activities took place there. Things like basket making, laundry, and food processing. The yard was swept often, a West African tradition passed to African American descendants. At the Big House, Thomas Livsey said the kids would go to the field to get broom sage for brush brooms to sweep the yard. This African tradition crossed cultures. My granny Freeman did the same thing in our yard. I, like Thomas, gathered broom sage in the field.

Broom Sage

Also, fresh sweet potatoes were stored in a dug-out hole covered in straw. We did this on our farm too. This pit, known as a vegetable kiln, is a traditional African method of storage. And barbeque...Cooking and roasting foods in fire pits and hot ashes originated in Africa and Caribbean (see the chapter *Pigs Smell Better Cooked*). It was brought to America and passed down through generations. The Livseys roasted peanuts, sweet potatoes and pigs this way.

After a few years, The Promised Land became the center of gravity for a growing black community. Mr. Livsey and his family were among the first black families to own such a large piece of property in the area. Other African American property owners like the Andersons, Echols, and Browns lived nearby. Thomas Anderson, the son of slaves, and his wife Ida Belle opened the first African American owned grocery store in the area in the 1930s. Thomas Anderson's father Franklin Bell Anderson was born into slavery on the Anderson plantation, Pleasant Valley, in 1854.

Owning land was important to Robert Livsey. He and Morena would leave their children land, because as Robert said, "they didn't make any more." The Livseys began dividing their land into one to five-acre lots for the children in the late 1950s. As an example, Mr. Livsey gave the lot where the barn stood to their daughter Sally and her husband Perry in 1961. Dividing up the land didn't mean he was through farming. He continued to farm the land until his death in 1965. Believe it or not, Mr. Livsey passed away while plowing with his tractor.

Morena and Robert Livsey - 50th Wedding Anniversary

The community was first known as Bethel because of the New Bethel African Methodist Episcopal church. New Bethel was founded in 1891 surrounded by former plantations and cotton fields. The congregation first began meeting in a house on the banks of the Yellow River. Early members were baptized in the river. "When the river rose," according to an early member, "the water came right on into the church. On those days we'd arrive early to sweep out the water." After one particularly long rainy spell my dad went down to New Bethel. He said the pews were floating. The water was so high they were bumping against the ceiling.

In a segregated South, New Bethel AME was more than just a house of worship. The only school for the community's black children was established there. Others were miles away, in DeKalb County or Lawrenceville. Today, Anderson-Livsey Elementary School, named after the two pioneers, is less than a quarter mile from the Big House. Mrs. Dorethia Livsey, Thomas' wife, is a lifelong educator. At this writing, Mrs. Livsey is in her late 80's, and still works every day at the school that bears her family's name.

Here's a picture is of Thomas and Dorethia on their wedding

day.

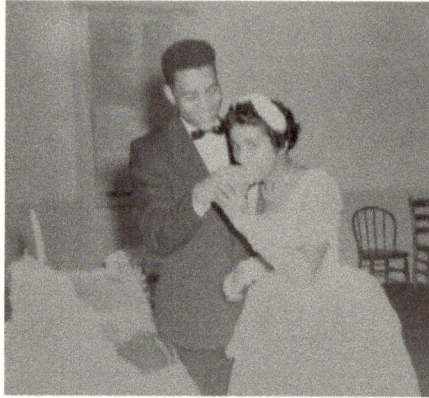

The Anderson and Livsey farms produced for their families and the community for decades. Thomas Livsey's business savvy and can-do spirit built The Promised Land into a thriving center of black life. As a young man, Mr. Livsey briefly left for Chicago. Then he served in the US Army in Korea. He came home to the family farm with a vision and a mission. Over the years, he built a small empire: 14 different homes for siblings and others, as well as a long list of businesses.

The Promised Land Grocery Store, opened in 1970. The strip mall had a barbershop, gas station, car wash, laundromat, and a restaurant.

The Promised land has seen changes in its almost 200-year history. The property was once a slave-worked plantation. Then it became a place where descendants of slaves could live, buy their own land, and not just survive but thrive. From a place of oppression to a sort of self-contained community. It was a rare place in rural Georgia where black people could be educated. Where they could become entrepreneurs, businesses owners, and build their own future. Today the area has devolved into a bedroom community for Atlanta. Yet, still, amid all that stands the Big House. A testament to the past, the present, and the future. God bless Robert Livsey, his son Thomas, and all those like them who kept their eye on the prize.

The house hasn't changed much since Thomas Maguire built it in 1825. The enclosed porch, and the rooms in the back are more recent additions, probably made by the Livsey family. Imagine opening that enclosed porch and removing the room additions. What's left is a "simple plantation" style house Some call houses like this a 4 up and 4 down, referring to the number of rooms on each floor.

The house had no indoor kitchen when it was built. Kitchens in the 19th century were separate buildings. This kept the kitchen heat somewhere else, and not in the house. Most country houses were wooden, so fire risk made separate kitchens a matter of safety too.

Mr. Maguire, an Irish immigrant, came to America in 1818. That's the same year Gwinnett County was carved out of Creek and Cherokee land. He won his first piece of property in 1820 land lottery. His lot was a fractional one, about 50 acres. The grant bordered the Hightower Trail on the southeastern side. The Hightower Trail was one of Georgia's many native trails. It ran from the Savannah River near present day Augusta to the mountains in the northwest part of the state. A spur trail runs off the Hightower Trail in a northeasterly direction. It was known as the Rock Bridge Trail. It connected the Hightower Trail to the Peachtree Trail north of present-day Lawrenceville. It was called Rock Bridge because of a granite shelf in the Yellow River at the site. That granite shelf made the river fordable most of the year. In the late 1600's, when Europeans first saw the trail and the rock bridge they asked the Creeks, "Who made this trail?" The natives told them trails were there when they got there. They said the "ancient ones" made them.

In 1825 after building his home, and getting things settled in Gwinnett County, Mr. Maguire returned to Ireland. He brought his family back to America. His parents, James and Catherine, settled in Augusta, and are buried in the Magnolia Cemetery there. His other relatives scattered themselves around the southeast. His brother, James, built a home in the area that became Rockbridge District. For a while that district was also called Maguire District.

Land was an important commodity and as such it was gobbled up as quick as it came available. Then came the gold rushes. The gold rushes in north Georgia and Sutter's Mill, California gave a few of Mr. Maguire's neighbors gold fever. They quickly sold their land and headed north or west. This enabled him to buy three lots of land that bordered his. Through the gold rush purchases, and others through the years, The Promised Land eventually grew to right at a thousand acres.

Thomas Maguire accomplished a lot at a young age. He was 17 when he arrived in America. Some folks speculate he brought money with him from Ireland. His parents may have given him seed money to help him get established. However, he came by it, he had it. The money bought land and human property as well. In the 1830 Census he owned 1 slave, in 1840 he had 12, in 1850 23, and by 1860 the number had risen to 26. In the economy of the antebellum South land, and the slaves to work it, equaled wealth. By both accounts Mr. Maguire was a wealthy man.

By 1830 he'd fulfilled all the obligations of a 19th century man. It was time to marry. Across the Yellow River was Pleasant Valley plantation, owned by Elijah Anderson. In 1830 Thomas married Jane Anderson. She and Mr. Maguire had 3 children. The marriage would end tragically. In 1837, while dismounting her horse, a rusty horse blanket pin scratched her leg. She developed blood poisoning and died. Jane's younger sister, Elizabeth, was sixteen when her sister died.

Thomas and Elizabeth Anderson Maguire

Mr. Maguire was grief-stricken. Elizabeth loved the children and felt sorry for them. Not surprisingly, just after her 17th birthday in 1838 she married Thomas. Elizabeth and Thomas had 8 children, making for 11 children in the household. For the time, a large family.

In 1834 The Maguire plantation became an election precinct. The same year a post office was established in Rockbridge. Mr. Maguire became the postmaster and held that office for 26 years. He was commissioned Captain of the Rockbridge district militia. In 1838 he represented Gwinnett County in the legislature. After the General Assembly provided for a public school system in Georgia, Thomas Maguire was appointed to the first county school board.

He was born into a Roman Catholic family, but in Gwinnett County he attended the Universalist Church. He also attended Rockbridge Baptist Church. He was a charter member of the

Lithonia Masonic Lodge Number 84 and was active in the Order of the Sons of Temperance. The Order of the Sons of Temperance was founded in 1842. It was fraternal, and had a benefit aspect, like todays Woodmen of the World. It's stated purpose was to free the drinking man from the slavery of alcohol. The Order was divided into Subordinate, Grand, and National Divisions. A pledge to total abstinence from strong drink was required from each member. To stay in communication, they had to refrain from manufacturing, purchasing, selling, or drinking all known and potential intoxicants. The benefits feature protected members and their families from hardships caused by sickness, unemployment, and death. Is it just me, or is the fact that Mr. Maguire had a Catholic upbringing, make his membership in the Order of the Sons of Temperance interesting.

Although Thomas Maguire was prominent citizen, he's best known for his farm journal. He kept the journal from 1859 to 1866, the seven most historic years of his life. It's known that he kept several journals, but only one has been copied. The Federal calvary took one. And recently one was found among a relative's papers. He wrote in longhand, but during the war with the scarcity of paper, he used shorthand. After the war the shorthand was transcribed, and the pages sewn together. The journal is 335 pages of 40 lines each.

The journal is detailed daily account of plantation life. In it he made notations of weather conditions, guests, and crops planted and harvested. Mr. Maguire allowed his slaves to attend church. This was highly unusual for slave owners. Most controlled the religious life of their slaves. They wanted to ensure that the message they received painted slavery as Godly and Biblical. One entry speaks of him taking his slaves to Rockbridge to hear a black preacher. He made the shoes for everyone on the plantation including slaves. This amounted to around thirty pairs a year. One entry says he completed eleven pairs of shoes in one day.

The story is told that Thomas Maguire named his plantation The Promised Land because the soil was so rich. It was self-sustaining with crops grown and skills learned. He, his sons, and the slaves did carpentry, blacksmithing, ginning, tanning of hides, milling of flour, grinding of cane, and making bricks. The plantation produced corn, cotton, wheat, vegetables, and fruit. They raised animals for slaughter, hogs, beef cattle, sheep, and chickens. The fields of The Promised Land were given names. There was Orchard, Farmer, Roundabout, Creek, Nelson, Trail, Moore, Freeman, Ford, Lee, Gin House, and School House. In November of 1862, two of his fields made 210 barrels, 26 wagon loads, and 25 cartloads of corn.

Let's face the truth, a slave is a human being in bondage. There's nothing good or pleasant about their situation. It's said that the Maguire slaves were treated decently but firmly. That usually means they were beaten if deemed necessary by the overseer or owner. According to the farm journal each slave family had their own garden patch. Mrs. McGuire tended to them when they were sick. They had shoes, clothing, medicine, Christmas gifts, and were allowed to celebrate holidays. At their death they received a decent burial.

Mr. Maguire was not a secessionist, but after Georgia seceded, he supported the Confederacy. He was 60 when the war started. Thus, he was too old for active duty. However, he studied military tactics and drilled new local recruits in basic military skills. In the journal he records that a group of ladies that came to The Promised Land to knit socks for the soldiers.

My 2nd great grandmother, Elizabeth Bryan Freeman, was in that group. They made 100 pair. News of the war was by word of mouth. Especially for the folks in southern Gwinnett County and Rockbridge. In the fall of 1864, word came that Sherman was burning Atlanta and marching eastward toward Augusta or Savannah. Although twenty miles from Atlanta, the people of The Promised Land could hear the boom of cannon fire and see the smoke from the burning.

Both Federal and Confederate soldiers raided the plantation. A sort of equal opportunity pillaging. Both sides slaughtered animals and took all the food they could find. As the war dragged on the South became increasingly desperate. Desertion was high, and supplies were almost nonexistent. Southern men, most of whom didn't own slaves, were tired of fighting a war to protect a way of life they'd never experience. Poor boys were dying while the children of the rich stayed safe at home and paid someone to fight for them. Not to mention that their wives and children were starving. At different times, hundreds of soldiers were camped in the fields and around the house. During Sherman's march Mr. Maguire and his son James hid in the woods for three weeks as they waited for the soldiers to leave. Although there's no explanation for it, the Big House wasn't burned. But his gin house, stables, barn, and fences were burned, and Union soldiers ate the family's livestock. Then they provisioned themselves for the march ahead.

By fall of 1864 everything the Maguire family had except their home and land were gone. Starvation was a real possibility. On top of that, although they had no money, they were still expected to pay taxes. Thomas Maguire bristled at the idea. He sent a list of 73 items to the Inferior Court of Gwinnett County. He knew exactly what was taken on July 22, 1864. He noted every missing thing in his journal. He hoped the loss would exempt the family from taxes for 1864. There was everything from six-hundred pounds of bacon ($2400) to a pound of pepper ($3). The grand total was $35,481.70. That's $687,321.21 in 2023. They denied his claim.

The people of The Promised Land, black and white, suffered during reconstruction. Since the journals for that period of Thomas Maguire's life are missing, we don't know specifics. Thomas Maguire died November 25, 1886.

THE HIGH PRICE PAID

Death, like a dank and misty veil, enshrouds the men of old.
Silence consumes them as they lie moldering in the ground.
Death's grip is tight, and his fingers provide no warmth against the cold.
Time marches over them as they lay stiffly in their tombs.
False glory is gone, vanished in the shadows of doom.

The sounds of the fray are silent now, the battle done.
A stillness has fallen over fields once covered in blood.
Both Blue and Gray have disappeared, like a bird that flies across the sun.
Where are their battle flags and their fiery combat lust?
Vanished. There's nothing left but dust.

Freedom's flowers now bloom on the battlefields where they fought.
They flourish around the whipping post, and the slave market.
No man could stand their ground against the judgement God has wrought.
No state could prosper if founded upon such sin.
A nations shame has finally seen the beginning of the end.

GRANNY FREEMAN'S OLD-FASHIONED CORNBREAD

Granny's cornbread requires a 10-inch cast-iron skillet. If you ain't got one, get one. Make sure your cast iron skillet is seasoned. If you don't know what that means, look it up. This cornbread is made with buttermilk, a true Southern staple. On top of that it's a quick and easy recipe!

Ingredients

- 4 tablespoons bacon grease divided (no substitutes allowed)
- 2 cups coarse stone-ground cornmeal (White-Lily corn meal is allowed, NO cornmeal mix)
- 1 teaspoon baking powder
- 1 teaspoon baking soda
- 1 teaspoon salt
- 2 large eggs

- 1-1/2 cups buttermilk

Instructions

1. Preheat the oven to 400 degrees Fahrenheit.
2. Add 2 tablespoons bacon grease to a 10-inch cast-iron skillet. Place the skillet in the oven for five to seven minutes to heat up.
3. While the skillet is heating up, combine the cornmeal, baking powder, baking soda, and salt in a large bowl and mix well.
4. Add the eggs, buttermilk, and 2 tablespoons melted bacon grease to a smaller bowl and whisk until well mixed.
5. Add the liquid ingredients to the dry ingredients and mix until just combined. Don't over mix.
6. Using a heavy-duty oven mitt or potholder, carefully remove the hot skillet from the oven. Tilt the skillet to make sure the bottom and sides are covered with oil. Immediately pour the batter into the skillet. You should hear a nice sizzle, and you'll see the batter start to rise.
7. Place the skillet back in the oven and bake for 20-25 minutes, or until the cornbread is a deep golden brown and has pulled away from the sides a little. To ensure it is done, insert a toothpick into the center. It should come out clean. Serve immediately.

More Stuff To Know About Granny's Cornbread

Cornbread will keep two to three days on your kitchen counter, about a week in the refrigerator, or about two to three months in the freezer. Be sure to wrap it tightly and keep it covered.

Leftover cornbread is delicious when sliced and toasted under the broiler for a minute. Top with as much butter as you like. Granny said you can never have too much butter.

If you don't have buttermilk, you can make your own. 1 cup of whole milk with 1 tablespoon of lemon juice or white vinegar. Let sit for five minutes, and you've got homemade buttermilk!

REVIVALS, FUNERAL HOME FANS, AND A SENSE OF BELONGING

For generations, folks all over the South have lived in 2 worlds: The world of their extended family and the world of their community. Within the family we have food, clothing, shelter, security, emotional support, help in times of trouble, and identity. How many times have I heard, "Ain't you Morris and Molly Freeman's boy?" Community is a location. In our community, we have a network of relationships with families and neighbors. We get along. Sometimes getting along is hard work, but it's better than killing each other.

The thing that holds a community together is a church. Some towns got their names and identity from a church. Others got their names from a certain accident of geography or geology. The latter only became a community after a church was established there. There're thousands of groves of pine and oak trees in the South. But Pine Grove or Oak Grove community are only called that because a church chose the feature for their name. Interestingly, Yellow River Baptist Church in Gwinnett County is located near the Yellow River. The settlement was there. The church took the name of the river, and so it goes.

As at Yellow River, the church was usually near the middle

of the settlement. When members walked to church or came by horse and buggy (or mule and wagon), that distance set the outer boundaries of the community. Next, the country schoolhouse was built nearby. Later, the church became a place to vote too. A few communities were blessed with more than one church. If so, the relationship between the churches was friendly. For example, the relationship between Rock Bridge Baptist Church (named for a ford of the Yellow River), and Zoar Methodist Church. For years these two churches in Centerville alternated Vacation Bible school. They did the same with revivals. The welfare of their people, and the community, led them to act with harmony and in unity. I grew up thinking the only difference between the Baptists and the Methodists is the price of the water bill. For you heathens, or members of other denominations, the Baptist dunk, and the Methodist sprinkle.

Church was the place where important things happened. There were holiday celebrations, especially Christmas. This too was an alternated event between Zoar and Rock Bridge. The birth of Jesus was dramatized, usually by the children. We'd struggle with Biblical language, and sometimes have live animals in the play. The uptown churches called their plays a pageant. Same thing. No child left without a present, some candy and oranges. We only had oranges around Christmas time. That was also true of soft, stick peppermint candy. When death visited a family, word sped through the grapevine. In Centerville, both churches rang their bells to announce a death. An avalanche of comfort, consolation and help came from every direction. In early times, the men of the 2 churches would gather at the proper graveyard (Rock Bridge or Zoar) and dig the grave. Someone in the community made the coffin. Marriages and births were also everyone's business and were celebrated. In a small village like ours, marriages sometimes tied families together in new ways.

Worship services in our churches were tough. There was no climate control. It was cold in winter and hot in summer. The heat came from a wood or coal-burning pot-bellied stove. Ours at Zoar was in the back corner. You can imagine how well it heated the whole church. That may be why Methodists won't sit on the front pew. These old stoves had to be fired early and stoked often in winter. Before the arrival of electricity, which came in the mid 1940's in Centerville, lighting came from Aladdin lamps hung from the ceiling.

They put out more light than the kerosene-burning lamps we used at home. The hanging lamps also had a wick and used kerosene. The difference was how the wick worked. Light from an Aladdin lamp wick shined on a pear-shaped mantel made of fiber. But, and there's always a but, if the wick wasn't adjusted just right, soot formed on the mantel, and it would fail. When they heard a soft "sputtering" sound, everyone sitting under that lamp vacated the pew. One of the men then hopped on the pew and readjusted the wick. Then the preacher had to readjust his sermon.

Even after the coming of the wires, it was years before Centerville's churches could afford air conditioning. Summer worship was just as uncomfortable as winter worship. The heat and humidity made it brutal. The only relief was to open the windows. Neither of our churches had screens. Screens would have helped with the flies, but not the temperature. The air that came through the windows at 11:30 A.M. in midsummer gave little relief. Open windows helped to move the air a little. That brings us to the wonderful hand-held funeral home fan.

A few of the most prosperous ladies had sturdy, fancy personal fans. However, funeral homes provided most of the fans we used.

This was both a service and advertising. Typically, they were made of stiff paper with a wooden handle. The handle reminded me of the wooden tongue compressors Dr. Willis McCurdy used. He'd always take one out of the Mason jar on his desk and take a gander down your throat. It didn't matter if you were there with a broken arm. He always looked. Back to the funeral home fans. One side featured a Biblical scene, perhaps the Resurrection, or the Garden of Gethsemane. Somewhere on the picture was a familiar Scripture verse. The verse may or may not have anything to do with the picture. For instance, the picture might be a very European looking Jesus knocking on a door. The Scripture? "Come unto me all ye who are weary and heavy laden, and I will give thee rest" (Matthew 11:28). The other side named the funeral home from whence this precious gift came. In August we were happy, yea, grateful to have them. As I said earlier, the heat and humidity were not the only summer plague. There were insects. In our area, north-central Georgia (or south-north Georgia depending on how you look at it) the culprits were mosquitoes and biting flies. The poor folks in South Georgia even now struggle with grey gnats, aka "no-seeums." These instruments of Satan can fly right through screens. They dart through open doors in a split second. The beasts crave moisture, so they like the eyes, ears, noses, and mouths. They bite too. My dad said they were nothing but wings and teeth. A true pestilence. The best available defense in both locales was the funeral home fan. The South Georgia folks call funeral home fans "gnat batters".

The second big event for churches, after the Christmas play, was the annual summer revival. The annual revival meeting is often held in August. This time was chosen for a reason. The season tobacco harvest was over. School hadn't started (at least back then). It wasn't time to pick cotton. Row crops were coming in, but not heavily. It was "slack time" or something like that. Yes friends, August down here is as hot as a 2-dollar pistol. Windows were opened, fans passed out. Papa Freeman said that the reason revival was in August was so the preachers could easily convince people of the terrors of hellfire. There were many positives to revivals. The hardest work in the field was done. Folks had time for neighbors, caught up on local goings on, and relaxed together. The settlement was reborn. The Gospel was reaffirmed.

Occasionally I like to take a stroll down memory lane. Lately I've thought a lot about worship in days gone by. I was just thinking about some of those experiences. Most folks today have no idea about those times. The world, and church life have changed over the years. In my youth, many rural church buildings had a sanctuary and maybe a couple of Sunday School rooms. There were other things I remember too, I'll call them "features." Here's a few.

Pew Pallets: Most churches didn't have nurseries. Our 2 in Centerville didn't. Instead, pew pallets were the norm. Parents spread quilts on the pew next to them.

Sometimes the quilts were put at the front of the sanctuary. Either way, infants and toddlers were laid upon them when they got sleepy. The services went right on. The singing and preaching never stopped. Yes, there was crying, and occasionally little ones crawling all over. God didn't seem to care. His Word wasn't hindered. People were saved, sanctified, and filled with the Holy Ghost depending on the denomination. The churches grew.

Open Windows: Like I said earlier, churches didn't have central heat and air. In the heat of summer, folks depended on funeral home fans and open windows. Window screens were rare, and bugs weren't. Many pastors have swallowed a bug or two while bringing the Word. Did the heat and humidity hinder the worship of God in those early days? Not at all. In fact, summer revivals were well attended. On some evenings people would be outside the building. They watched and worshiped through the open windows.

Simplicity: I remember when a sweet, little old lady, who was a member of our church died. She was widow (or widder) and had very little money.

Wisely, she planned, and made sure her favorite color was center stage. One of the carpenters in the church made her a beautiful pine casket. It was draped with a red tablecloth instead of flowers. She was dressed in her favorite red house dress. After the service the pallbearers loaded her into the back of a red pickup truck. They all climbed in, 3 on one side, and 3 on the other. The truck was followed to the cemetery by the procession of mourners. Each vehicle had their lights on, and a red ribbon tied to its antenna. Upon arrival at the cemetery, the pallbearers carried her to, and lowered her into, the grave. The men of the church had dug the grave. She was a kind woman and I know her simple ceremony made her smile.

Dinner on the Ground:

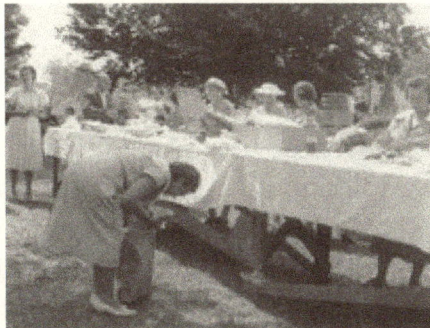

Before fellowship halls and family life centers, churches had potluck dinners. They just happened outside. Churches were often surrounded by big oak trees. Between those trees were chest high tables nailed to the tree trunks. In Centerville the tables were made of local granite. On the days of the potlucks, members cooked for "dinner on the ground," a churchwide picnic. Most ladies had their "dishes", and it wasn't cool to make a dish someone else was known for. Often these dinners were at the beginning or end of the revival. Many times, they were called "Homecoming." Past members were invited and usually attended, at least on the day of the dinner on the ground. The tables were covered with food. Being outside, this required "fanners." Fanners were stationed around the tables and fanned the food constantly. Yes, the funeral home fans came in handy again. This served as a poor fly deterrent, but it's all they had. Once you filled your plate, flies became a personal problem. Another difference I've noticed, back then the older folks were served first. If they were mobile, they went through the line. If they couldn't walk, someone got their food for them. Today it seems the children are the priority. Many other things quite different too, but what hasn't changed?

Change Ain't Always Bad: As a rule, most of us don't like change. Many of us even resist change. Hey, listen at my age I get it. But I was just thinking, not all change is bad. It's fun to reminisce, but most wouldn't want to return to "the good ole days." The days of pew pallets, open windows, bugs, and funeral home fans. However, since Christians are always ready to eat, dinner on the ground will always be welcomed! Even if it's in a nice, air-conditioned fellowship hall.

We Southerners have a need to belong. The need, for us at least, is tied to family and community. The great Southern author, Thomas Wolfe, wrote a book titled *You Can't Go Home Again.* I beg to differ. Home is the only place you can go. It'll never again be the way your memories see it, but it will always be home.

MOM'S CANDIED SWEET POTATOES

This recipe was another of my mother's go-to items for a Homecoming, or dinner on the ground. It's sweet enough to be a desert.

Ingredients

- 2 cups white sugar
- 1 teaspoon ground cinnamon
- 1 teaspoon ground nutmeg
- 1 pinch salt
- 1/2 cup butter
- 6 sweet potatoes, peeled and sliced
- 1 tablespoon vanilla extract

Instructions

1. In a small bowl, mix the sugar, cinnamon, nutmeg, and salt together.

2. Melt butter in a large skillet over medium heat; add sweet potatoes and stir to coat.
3. Sprinkle sugar mixture over the sweet potatoes and stir.
4. Cover skillet and reduce heat to low.
5. Cook, stirring occasionally, for 1 hour, or until the sauce is dark and the potatoes are candied.
6. They should be tender, but a little hard around the edges.
7. Stir in vanilla and serve.

MY FIRST CHRISTMAS WITHOUT POP

My dad was my hero. I'm sure that's true for a lot of men. He was always strong, and independent. But after his stroke in 2016 that all changed. As he steadily declined the roles were reversed. I had to be strong. I had to do things for him that I never dreamed I would do. I did them gladly. One little story, if you'll indulge me.

On top of everything else he had going on, he had glaucoma. That required eye drops every night before bed. I'd open the door to where he and mom were sitting watching TV. As I opened it, I'd say, "Leroy," in a high-pitched voice. He'd answer, "Yes," also in a high-pitched voice. Then I'd say (high-pitched voice), "I've come to pee in your eyes." He'd laugh and say OK. I'd do the deed and lean over and kiss him on the forehead. He'd grab my shoulders and say, "Boy, you'll never know how much I love you." I'd always tell him I loved him too. This was our every night ritual for the last 2 years of his life. Pop was wrong. I did know how much he loved me. How, you say? Well, I have a son of my own, and I know how much I love him.

The sun is sinking low
as Christmas takes its leave.
Another year has almost gone.
to loved ones, we must cleave.

Memories flood my heart
of those who've gone before.

Tears and laughter mingle; could
I have loved him more?

God's fire light's the Western sky
as the sun passes from view.
My thoughts turn to happy times,
and my memories of you.

You left me suddenly this summer.
Your noble heart ceased to beat.
You went quietly like you lived,
and fell softly at Jesus' feet.

In my heart of hearts, I know
that our separation won't be long,
but Dad it's hard. I miss you Pop.
I can't believe you're gone.

Thank God for the eternal light
that shone brightly in your breast.
That light will guide me homeward
until we're together again at rest.

Your Loving Son, Terry
Christmas Day, 2019
Nathaniel Morris Freeman
1930 - 2019

GRANNY FREEMAN LIVED A QUIET LIFE

Her full name was Ila Maude Campbell Freeman. She was a Godly woman, a life-long Missionary Baptist. She only left the state of Georgia once in her lifetime. She was an amazing woman. Let me tell you more about her.

Ila Maude Campbell came into this world on August 6, 1887. She was born at the Campbell homeplace on the corner of Johnson Road and Campbell Road in Centerville, Gwinnett County, Georgia. The old house is long gone. Until about 8 years ago one of the outbuildings was still standing. Now it's gone too. Granny was the second child of 11, 6 boys and 5 girls. Her parents were James William "Uncle Billy" Campbell and Shady Ann Clower. Neither of whom ever left the confines of the county.

The photo is Shady and Uncle Billy, Granny's parents. They're sitting in front of the homeplace.

Think about that birth-year for a minute. 1887. That was before cars, tractors, and airplanes. They had no electricity, no running water, and no indoor plumbing. Radio and TV were way out in the future. Electricity didn't come until Roosevelt's New Deal created the REA, Rural Electric Authority. Our local co-op organized in 1936. Big city's got electric power in the late 1800's. The reason rural areas didn't was the expense. The cost of running lines was about $2,000 a mile in the 1930s. The power companies couldn't make any money at that cost per mile. Especially selling electricity to widely spread-out farms. The REA made low-cost loans to farmers living in roughly the same area. Each group then formed an electric "cooperative". A cooperative is owned and operated by the people it serves. With the government money the co-op could build lines and other infrastructure. Then they sold the power to members to repay the loans. It worked. The Campbell homeplace got wires in the 1940's.

Granny Freeman never attended school. They saw no need for a girl to do so. It's hard for us sophisticated, 21st century folks, to wrap our heads around the concept on no school for girls. Anyway, public schools were very hit or miss in Georgia until 1949. This was especially true in rural areas. If they had access to schools at all, most only met 3 or 4 months out of the year. Boys went just long enough to get some basic math skills. In the late 19th / early 20th century everyone was expected to work. And work they did.

Chores were plentiful. Based on conversations I had with Granny in the late 70's here's what a typical day on the Campbell farm looked like. Before daylight, some of the girls helped their mother fix breakfast. This started very young. It's where the cooking education began. The others fed, watered, and milked the goats. They rotated each morning. They helped wash the dishes, clean the house, and keep the yard swept clean. The girls learned to sew, crochet, and knit. They learned how to can fruit and vegetables and make jellies and jams. They helped with dinner and supper too. In the evening the girls went to the henhouse and gathered the eggs.

They were taught how to do laundry, or as Granny called it, "wersh clothes." Clothes washing was a chore in and of itself and was done once every 2 weeks. First, they built a fire under a black iron cauldron. The same one they used at hog killing time. When the water got good and hot, in went the clothes. They stirred them until they were completely soaked, took them out, and scrubbed them with homemade lye soap on a washboard. After a good scrubbing they went back into the pot for more stirring. After the second stirring the clothes were taken out again. The clothes were then rinsed in a pot of clean water. Granny said the hardest part of wash day for her was wringing the clothes. Once wrung out, the clean garments were hung on the clothesline to dry. It was an all-day job. When the clothes dried, they were folded and put up. It makes me tired just writing about it.

The boys started young too. They learned to feed and milk the cow. The mule had to be fed and watered every day. At planting and harvest time, he had to be put into and taken out of the harness. They learned how to plow the fields. The Campbell boys fed and watered the chickens too. They helped their daddy fix any problems with the goat and chicken pens. They helped him look for signs of chicken predators and make any necessary repairs to the house.

I asked Granny how this work was divided up. She broke it down by age. My notes are faded, but here's a stab at what she said:

Ages 2-3:

- Gather eggs,
- Brush goats,
- Pick up sticks in yard,
- Pick up rocks in the garden.

Ages 4-5:

- All the above, plus...
- Feed small animals.
- Bottle feed baby animals.
- Plant seeds,
- Water garden,
- Sweep yard.

Ages 6-7:

- All the above, plus...
- Water animals,
- Rake leaves,
- Brush mule and cow,
- Weed garden,
- Wash the windows,
- Help on wash day,
- Hang laundry on clothesline,
- Fold and put away dry clothes,
- Sweep the porches.

Ages 8-9:

- All the above, plus...
- Pick fruit and vegetables,
- Feed larger animals,
- Milk goats
- Paint

Ages 10-11:

- All the above, plus...
- Plow and plant the garden,
- Hoe the garden,
- Milk cow,
- Organize tools and keep them clean and sharp,

- Trim hooves of small animals,
- Scrub and clean animal feeders.

Ages 12 and up:

- All the above, plus...
- Trim hooves of large animals,
- Help deliver baby animals,
- Plow and hoe the garden.

All these things, and anything else on the farm that needed doing! There wasn't much time for play, but they somehow found time. The boys played marbles, mumbley-peg with a pocketknife, they carved tops out of blocks of wood, and made ball and cup games to play with. The girls favored dolls. Granny said her favorite doll was a corn shuck doll. Her daddy made it as a gift for her 3rd birthday. She still had it when she married. Speaking of marriage...

Ila Maude Campbell married Nathaniel Sephus Freeman on July 29, 1906. They met at Rockbridge Baptist Church. Granny was a faithful member there. She walked to church. It was only about a half mile from her house. I think Papa started attending when he was courting Granny. I'm sure she insisted he do so. They were the same age when they married, almost. Both were 18. Papa had been 18 for a couple of months. Granny

was 8 days short of her 19th birthday. July 29, 1906, fell on a Sunday. Papa plowed in his daddy's fields from daylight to dinner time. Granny, as was her practice, went to church. The wedding was at 3 PM. They left right after the service for their new rented home on Centerville-Rosebud Road. He bought a new oak bedroom suite for Granny as a wedding present. It was already at the house, and surprised Granny. I still have that suite. He paid $15.00 for a dresser, chest of drawers, and an iron bedstead and bedding. That house on Centerville-Rosebud Road would be their home until they bought their own place in 1924. In that little rental house 5 of their 6 children were born, all girls. My Dad, the only boy, was born at the "new" house on Zoar Church Road.

Their first born was a cutie named Ila Mae. She came in September of 1907. The stork stayed away until December 1912. Her name was Easter Lois. Lucy Belle entered this world in late September 1914. Granny bore 3 girls in 9 years, a decent pace for that time, and a woman od her age. A beautiful time turned painful in May 1915.

Little 2-and-a-half-year-old Easter Lois took sick in late April. What started as a cold quickly became something much worse. She died on May 2nd. Granny and Papa were devastated. Papa didn't want his family to be buried at Rockbridge near his daddy. He rode the mule over to Mr. J. W. Starnes house. Mr. Starnes was one of the trustees at Zoar. Papa bought a 3-grave plot at Zoar Methodist church's graveyard. Easter Lois

was laid to rest in that plot on the morning of May 4th, 1915. Papa made her little wooden coffin. The men of Zoar and Rockbridge dug the grave. Children dying was not uncommon in the early 1900's. Even so, in a small rural community like Centerville it affected everyone. Granny said that folks treated her kindly during the mourning period, but differently. She felt like folks were, as she said, "a little bit tip-toey" around her. That all changed when Susie Marie was born March 23, 1918. 2 years later Opal Jeanette came along. That's the 5 girls Granny Freeman bore in the rental house.

Granny's life on the farm wasn't much different than her mothers. Chores, raising young'uns, raising Papa, and going to church. They still didn't have the modern amenities, but they were happy. Granny taught herself to read so she could read her Bible. It was a hard life, but a good one. In a later chapter I'll be writing about the land. Having land of your own was as big a deal then as it is now. I want to tell you how it changed the family's life. But not now…

When I sat down to write this chapter, I wanted to catch the essence of my granny Freeman. But what do you say about a life that was lived in the background? A life that had no interests outside of her God, family, and friends. Someone who was content to sit in her rocker on the porch after chores. Just rocking and watching the breeze scatter the leaves off the elm tree around the yard.

Today when famous people pass away, they wind up on our

screens. That'd be computer, laptop, tablet, phone, or TV screens We see short video clips or obituaries documenting their achievements. The talking heads on the news discuss their impact and influence. The quiet lives, though, pass on soundlessly. And yet, those lives are in our skin. Their example guides us from breakfast to bed. Their lives made us, and our world, and they keep that world turning. Folks like Granny take the trash to the burn barrel before we notice it needs doing. She walks out to the mailbox to see if the mail has run. She shows us how to roll out the biscuit dough to just the right thickness. Granny took our son up on her lap when he was just a little shaver. Granny helped the neighbors with their canning, and at hog killing time. She slipped money into my pocket before I went on a date. She did our laundry because mother worked in Atlanta. She kept the house and played in the yard with me like a kid. Granny and Papa split a sleeve of soda crackers and climbed into bed night after night. They did so until all their nights were used up. People like Granny leave people behind who carry on living. Because making a life on a piece of land on Zoar Church Road is important. It was important to her, and her life made it important to us.

All around us are these lives. Lives like Granny's. Folks with their heads down but their arms wide open. They ignore the temptress of flashy American individualism. Shunning the bright lights and accolades. Like Granny Freeman they say, "I'm fine right here at the edge of the room. I don't need to be in the center." To our 21st century sensibilities that contentment is somewhat subversive. The world demands to know how can you just want that? There's more to life, always more, or so "they" say.

My granny Freeman died on May 29, 1982. She died like she lived, quietly.

Granny's heath began declining in her 92nd year, and she had to go into the hospital for the first time. She was tough as nails. I never heard a word of complaint cross her lips. I know she must had had complaints. We all do, the older we get. Papa died in 1970, so she had 12 years without her first and only love. 12 years of sleeping alone for the first time since she was 18 years old. The illness caused her to lose her ability to walk. Mom and Dad couldn't take care of her at home so sadly we had to put her in a nursing home. That was tough for us all, especially Granny. Dad's sister, my aunt Marie, got Granny out of the nursing home. She and Uncle Tink brought her their house. She lived about 2 weeks after that.

The day Granny passed my wife, my son, and I went to Aunt Marie's. Judy was a nurse and she wanted to monitor Granny. She'd been unable to speak for several days and took a downturn the evening of May 28th. We all knew it wouldn't be long. Mom and Dad were in Florida. They needed a break and I insisted they get away for a while. I had no idea how bad they needed to get away at the time. I do now, after taking care of them for almost six years.

Nate was 4 years old, much too young to grasp what was going on. Judy went inside to sit with Granny. I kept Nate outside playing in the yard. My precious wife sat beside Granny's bed with her stethoscope on Granny's chest listening to her heartbeat. It grew fainter and fainter, and then fell silent. She was gone. My living aunts were there too. There were tears, and hugs all around. Judy made her way outside to tell me. I lost it. She watched Nate until I regained my composure, then she went back inside. Soon the fire truck arrived. This is common practice when someone dies at home unless hospice is involved. Next came the hearse. I did fine with the fire truck. It fascinated my little boy, so all that was cool. But with the hearse, the questions started coming. "Who's that Daddy?" "Why are they here?" "What's that wagon they're taking in?" "What are they doing?" I answered them all as best I could, but that last one. What do you tell a 4-year-old about the complexities, and nuances of the Christian death ritual? I finally said, "They've come to take Granny and make her pretty." He looked up at me and said, "They don't need to do that Daddy. Granny's already pretty." I totally lost it. I'm tearing up now, 41 years later.

What got to me then, and now, was the truth in what he said. Sure, there was grief and sadness, but that kernel of truth exploded in my heart. Granny Freeman was pretty, no, she was beautiful, inside and out.

GRANNY'S PAN-FRIED OKRA

Crispy and crunchy on the outside yet tender on the inside with just the right sprinkle of salt. Buy extra because your family will eat this fried okra up! Have you got that cast iron skillet yet? You're going to need it for this recipe too.

Ingredients

- 3 cups washed and sliced fresh okra

- 1/2 cup homemade butter milk - (½ cup milk with 1 tablespoon white vinegar)

- 1 cup cornmeal

- 1/4 cup flour

- 1 tablespoon salt

- 1/4 teaspoon pepper

- Bacon grease, or vegetable oil for frying

Instructions

1. To make buttermilk add vinegar to milk and let sit

for 5 minutes.

2. Mix cornmeal, flour, salt, and pepper in a bowl.
3. Heat oil in cast iron skillet.
4. Place okra in a large bowl and pour buttermilk on top of okra.
5. Gently mix okra and buttermilk. Then strain okra in a mesh colander.
6. Gently add okra to dry ingredients, turning to coat.
7. When oil is hot (test by dropping a small amount of cornmeal into grease & if it starts to sizzle, oil is ready) shake off excess cornmeal on okra and add to skillet. Do not touch the okra for at least 6 minutes.
8. Carefully turn okra and continue to cook for approximately 6 to 8 minutes on medium heat until brown.
9. Place on paper towels to drain and sprinkle with salt.

THE FOOL

He stood alone on the street that night
with a cold rain falling down.
Trembling in the shadows of the only streetlight
in a dangerous part of town.

It was almost midnight and the day shunners
were starting to move about.
His cardboard signs letters were running.
He was crazy, I had no doubt.

Well, I've always been the curious type
and this man was strangely intriguing.
So, I pulled up my collar as I lit my pipe
when to my surprise he started singing.

It was a song I knew from long ago.
I'd heard it in Sunday School.
"Jesus loves me," he sang very low.
I just stopped and stared at the fool.

People ignored him and kept their pace.
He just looked at them and smiled.
The expression on the dude's face
reminded me of a child.

I ambled on over and leaned on the wall
just to listen for a while.
Curses and threats came from any and all,
but his reaction was meek and mild.

I stood and watched for as long as I dared,

then stepped from my dark place into the light.
I said, "Man did you really think anyone cared?
You ain't changing the world on this street tonight."

My question was loud, but it wasn't fake.
He turned and wiped the rain from his eyes to see.
He said, "I suppose not friend, I just want to make
sure that it doesn't change me."

WATERMELON, BOYHOOD, AND "PLACE"

Watermelon right out of the cooler on a hot summer day. Yes, a very juicy, perfectly ripe, ice-cold watermelon. How about the aroma of a blackberry cobbler baking in the oven. What's better than the taste of home-made peach ice cream, especially the part that sticks to the dasher. The smell of Dad's pipe tobacco, Borkum Riff or Cherry Blend. The smoke from his Tampa Nuggets smelt wonderful too. The smell of leaves burning on a cool fall day. These things, and hundreds more, evoke powerful, life-defining memories. But more than that, they give us a sense of place. A place where we belong.

I have a compost pile. It's mostly unused, but I have one just in case. Judy and I had just finished one of those ice-cold watermelons. I put the rinds and seeds in a bowl and headed for the compost pile. As happens often, my mind began to wander. Suddenly, I wasn't in my backyard anymore. I was back to my childhood days, on the farm in Centerville, Gwinnett County, Georgia. There, summer days were spent playing in the woods, chasing baseballs, and working the fields.

Folks today would say we were poor and a bit rough. I disagree. We were country dwelling rural folk. No better, or no worse off than our neighbors. Air conditioning, cell phones, color tv, space travel and "new" clothes were imaginary things in our world. Money was usually in short supply. Yet, those times were the best. Except for the few times I had to fetch a switch for a whipping. Looking back, I usually deserved it, but that didn't make it fun. And the sweet freedom. Freedom to run and play without fear of mean people with bad intent. Playing baseball in the pasture, racing my cousin, Wanda, in the Daytona 500 around the elm tree, and "riding" a limber pine tree pretending to be on an elephant's back. What could be better than all that?

Mr. Floyd and Mrs. Kate Johnson were our neighbors across the field. Mrs. Kate was one of our lunchroom ladies at the school. Mr. Floyd drove our school bus, farmed, and did a little building to fill in the gaps. Most of the boys in Centerville worked for Mr. Floyd at one time or another, including me. The worst job I ever did for him was sacking wheat on the combine. It was hot, dusty, and non-stop. It's amazing how fast a 50-pound sack fills up. When the croaker sack is full you must tie it off, pick it up and drop it down the chute, and get another sack under the spout. Did I mention it never stopped?

One of the favorite jobs I had was picking watermelons. Almost every day we'd pick and sort them for Mr. Johnson to take to market. Some days we'd just about fill up the back of his old Ford pick-up. Other times, we had so many that we'd "bust" one open, wash our hands in it and "bust" open several more to eat. We only ate "the heart", the best part in the center. We threw away the rest. We filled our bellies. What a feast! Mr. Johnson had pigs, and so did we. We'd take some of the watermelons that weren't sellable and give them to his pigs. Pigs will eat most anything, but watermelons, swine love them. I can still hear the grunts and ear-piercing squeals. If there were enough, he'd let me take some home to our pigs. Yep, every living thing enjoys a good watermelon.

Sense of place is very important in the South. Just think

about "place" in Southern literature. It's important for both the writer and the reader. For the writer, a sense of place embodies a time and a place. It can also provide a starting point for developing characters' ideals, motivations, and actions. For the reader, a sense of place offers an empathy for an area and the basic workings of a culture. For instance, Harper Lee's *To Kill a Mockingbird* wouldn't be the same set in California, or the Bronx. Its descriptions of Great Depression Alabama and its unmitigated racism just wouldn't ring true. Likewise, what would Robert Penn Warren's *All the Kings Men* be if was set anywhere other than the deep South?

Even so, place and time are important for Northerners, Mid-Westerners, and Westerners. However, place and time don't seem near as important them as they are to us Southerners. We connect to place on another level. We and cling to our surroundings, its intricacies, and its nuances at an early age. We may reject them for a while as adults while we're attempting to find out who we are. However, almost without fail we return to them and embrace them as our journey unfolds.

It's evident to me that "place" creates an emotional response in us. The geographic location of the place and the time we associate with it. The Gwinnett County I know today is not the Gwinnett County of the 1950s, 60's, and 70's. It doesn't evoke the same emotions it did when I was growing up. The people and culture of the area have changed so much.

Speaking of emotions brought on by a place and time... One of those places for me is the once dilapidated, now renovated homeplace. I'm as connected to it, even in its current state, as I was when I was a child. It offers me the simplicity of a life so different from today. I can get lost in the good feelings of those days. Mr. Brady built the house in the 1880's. When Papa Freeman bought it in 1924 it had 3 rooms. It came with 62 acres of farmland. Dad was born there in 1930. My dad added 3 more rooms, and a bathroom it 1956. It was the first time Papa and Granny had indoor plumbing. It would remain the family home until 1963 and stay in the extended family until 2015.

I first saw the house in October 1952, although I have no memory of it. Before the remodeling in 1956 I vaguely remember it was delightfully imperfect. 3 rooms, and floorboard gaps that you could see right through to the ground. Granny Freeman told me she used to sit with me on the floor. We'd drop corn through the cracks for the chickens. When they'd grab the kernels, she said I'd cackle just like the chickens. The house had a small front porch, and a tiny back porch before the remodel. Dad screened in the front porch, enlarged the back porch, and added 3 rooms. Guess who did the remodeling work? That's right, Mr. Floyd Johnson. I guess, to most people, this description sounds like it was nothing more than a hovel. I guess on some level it was a hovel. But my grandmother was strict about its cleanliness and presentation. Me? I felt the safest there of anywhere I've ever been in the world.

There, the outside world couldn't penetrate. There, the morning smell of hot biscuits, frying sausage, and coffee awoke me to comfort. There, stories told until the wee hours of the morning sparked my imagination and filled me with wonder. The quartet Dad sang with practicing in the living room. The tongue-and-groove walls in white, pale green, and powder blue were a fortress. A chair by the fireplace in the dining room, along with a book, was a wonderful place on a cold winter day. The metal spring bed in Papa and Granny's room invited afternoon naps. The swing on the front porch's gentle rocking was soothing, its chains played a slow, clanking serenade. A massive elm tree in the front yard provided cool shade for the house, and a great place to play, even on red dusty summer days.

The front yard was grassless beige sand, swept clean. The

octopus-like tentacles of roots from the big elm became places to play with toy cars. We played mumbley-peg and marbles there. One side of the house was Granny's flower garden. She had irises, a mock orange that, in bloom, smelled like a bowl of Florida's finest oranges. She loved the sweet perfume of her gardenia bush, and color of the yellow bells in early spring. And standing guard over it all, that old elm tree. That old tree shaded us from the summer sun. And somehow it seemed to protect us from the drastic and stressful things happening in the outside world. Could I be so sheltered again? I would bow on my knees in deepest gratitude.

By the time my aunt Betty passed in 2008, it was unfit for habitation. She and Mom's brother, Uncle Willis, still owned the house. But they moved up to Jasper, Georgia in the early 2000's. My cousins hung on to the house until 2015. By then, Papa and Granny's room on the back had been open to the sky for about 10 years. The back porch, and bathroom were rotten. The beautiful old elm was dead, and its limbs were falling down every time the wind blew. Collapse of the old structure was imminent. Thankfully, the new owner has restored it completely.

Its condition didn't matter to me. I'd stand in the road and look at the sagging roof behind the dead elm. All I felt were the days of my childhood. A deep longing to return to an easy time when it seemed everything would be as it was eternally overwhelmed me. Even in its ramshackle death throes, it offered a respite for my weary heart and mind. That's the power of a sense of place, both in real life and on paper.

FREEMAN'S BLACKBERRY, OR DEWBERRY COBBLER

Blackberry cobbler is a delicacy. It's another desert we had often in the summer. Blackberries grow wild in Georgia, dewberries too. What are dewberries, you ask? The dewberry plant is a trailing vine. They grow lower to the ground like raspberries, instead of on upright vines like blackberries. You can find them most anywhere in the South, from Texas to Florida. Either one makes a tongue-slapping treat.

Ingredients

- ½ cup plus 2 tablespoons melted butter
- 1 cup self-rising flour
- 1 ½ cups sugar

- 1 cup whole milk
- 1-quart blackberries or dewberries
- ½ teaspoon vanilla extract

Instructions

1. Preheat oven to 350 degrees.
2. Melt butter and pour 1/2 cup into an 8-inch square baking dish.
3. In a small bowl combine flour, 1 cup sugar, milk, and vanilla until blended well.
4. In another bowl combine berries (black or dew) and remaining ½ cup sugar, and 2 tablespoons of melted butter; toss well.
5. Spoon berry mixture over batter.
6. Place in oven, and bake for 45 to 50 minutes, until top is golden brown, and the berries are tender.

Serve immediately. We always added a scoop of vanilla ice cream for good measure.

MEMORIAL DAY, ARLINGTON NATIONAL CEMETERY

Dawn approaches in the garden of stones.
Row upon row in its soft golden light.
Like spirits they rise in the distance
As day overcomes the night.

Each stone over a mother's son
or daughter, many fallen in foreign lands.
Weeping has passed, but it's always close.
Pictures in a book; clay imprints of little hands.

A nation's youth gone, like mist in the sun.
Sent to fight and die, and their mothers prayed.
Never forget the price paid with their blood.
Remember them always, and today.

DAYTONA BEACH MEMORIES

I was a fortunate boy. My parents took me to Florida on vacation every year. Not just to Florida, but Daytona Beach, Florida. That's right, The World's Most Famous Beach, at least that's their slogan. I had friends at school that never went on vacation. Like I said, I was fortunate. Both my parents had good jobs in Atlanta. Not everyone had that blessing.

My first trip to Daytona Beach was in December 1952. I was less than 2 months old. Mom said we stayed a week, and Dad dipped my feet in the ocean. I took her word for that. I have no recollection. You see, my parents loved Daytona Beach. It was like Shangri-La to them. They were still just kids. Dad was just barely 22. Mom was 20. Sand and surf had an alure, and it was embedded deep in their hearts. Dad loved to ride canvas rafts and body surf. Mom preferred a towel on the sand and a tan. Me? Well, I came to love it too, but in 1952 the most exciting thing to me was pooping my pants and a diaper change. Too much? Oh well, it's true.

I have so many memories of Daytona Beach. I plan to share them all, or at least those I can remember. So, sit back, relax, have a beverage if you're so inclined. Here we go.

We always made the trek in July. Mom and Dad's anniversary was July 4th. Both came from homes that weren't air-conditioned. Heck, central air didn't become a thing until the late 1960's. That's according to the U. S. Department of Energy.

I hate to tell them, but it was much later than that at our house. Anyway, Mom and Dad loved the heat. They figured with the ocean and the pool you could stay cool. At night, the ocean breeze through the jalousie windows, and the ever-present oscillating pedestal fan made it tolerable. Never heard of jalousie windows?

The picture shows a set. As you can see, a jalousie window had parallel glass panes. They were worked with a crank. You turned it one way to open and the other way to close. Not very energy efficient, but great at allowing air flow.

We always went to the beach with two other families, the Garners, and the McCullers. They had all boys, so our group was all boys. There was Dwight, Nicky, and Richie Garner, and Kenneth, Sammy, and Scotty McCullers. I barely remember Dwight and Kenneth, at least in Daytona. They were older, and soon went on to other pursuits. The rest of us were fast friends. Nicky and Sammy ran together, and Richie, me, and Scotty ran together. Scotty was the youngest, and looking back, he took way more junk than he should've. Kids can be mean, and I'm sorry to say we were.

The days before Interstate highways were awesome. We'd leave on Friday night around 6 P.M. after the adults got home from work. Our car was quickly loaded, and off we went. We could get away fast because Mom packed days ahead. A habit she took to her grave. We hooked-up with the Garners and McCullers down the road. There were no cellphones, so the meeting place was prearranged. I know we went south on U.S. Highway 441 and then swung over to Fargo Georgia. Usually, somewhere south of Dublin, Georgia I'd get sleepy. My routine went like this, grab a beach towel and my pillow, climb up on the package shelf, and fall asleep looking at the stars through the back window. Hey, the car didn't have seatbelts! Dad kept to the backroads until we picked up A1A north of Jacksonville, Florida. We stayed on A1A the rest of the way. We kids were looking for one thing, the ferry across the Saint Johns River at Mayport, Florida.

It was so cool to drive onto that ferry and head out onto the river. Wide awake now, I stayed glued to the oceanside window. The air smelt like Sulphur, or rotten eggs. Around Saint Augustine, Florida the sun came up. It was glorious.

Our first serious stop, other than pee breaks on the side of the road, was Fort San Marcos. Its official name is the Castillo de San Marcos, the Castle of Saint Mark. The old Fort is on St. Augustine's Matanzas Bay. It's a bastion-style fortress and was established as a military post in 1672. The Spanish built the fort from an indigenous stone called coquina. The rock is formed by the shells of dead shellfish, and it's tough. Coquina absorbs cannonballs instead of being shattered by them. The Spanish had no idea.

The Garners at the Castillo

Coquina is what they had, so that's what they used. The Castillo is the only 17th-century military structure in the nation, and it's the oldest U.S. masonry fortress. A cool place. The adults sat in the shade and had a smoke while we kids went wild. Running up and down the stairs to the cannons where we fired at pirate ships and Yankee gunboats. When we got good and tired, they'd round us up. Back in the cars and we'd head across the Bridge of Lions and turn south toward Daytona Beach.

For an adventurous boy, Daytona Beach had it all. A Boardwalk with rides and games. Skeeball, my favorite, was 5-cents for 9 balls. There was a long fishing pier. The boardwalk also had several saltwater taffy stores. One had a machine in the window that pulled the taffy. Fascinating. We fished from the pier at least once while we were there. The only thing I remember catching is saltwater catfish. A bandshell with

bands and fireworks, especially on the 4th of July. The ocean was a playground, you could ride waves, and chase Round Sardinella in the surf. There was digging for Sand Fleas, building sandcastles, and burying each other in the sand.

And the ice cream truck, the glorious ice cream truck. There were several who ran up and down beach. They all played *Turkey in the Straw* over their loudspeaker obnoxiously loud. You could hear them coming, for sure. Kids would beg for a quarter and run to meet the truck. 25-cents got you a single-stick popsicle. Our favorite flavor was grape. You could tell what flavor other kids had by the color of their lips.

It seemed like a Steak and Shake was on every corner. Us guys loved Steak and Shake.

We ate there every time our parents let us. That was usually 2 or 3 times a week, and always in the evenings. You see, they liked to go see Brother Dave Gardner or the Ink Spots at one of the clubs in town. They saw the Mills Brothers once, and Dean Martin and Jerry Lewis. Dad couldn't stand Jerry Lewis. He thought he was silly. Anyway, Steak and Shake had the best hamburgers. They fried them on a flattop and used the spatula to flatten them out. This let the juices crisp up around the edges. I always got a double cheeseburger because they put the cheese between the 2 pieces of meat. When they pressed it down, the cheese and the juices mingled. Oh my, that was some good eating. My mouth is watering as I write this. The fries were small and long and always hot when they got to the table. My drink of choice was a large chocolate malt, although I did have a cherry coke once and awhile. Our lunches at the motel consisted of bologna and cheese sandwiches and chips. That delicacy was washed down with a 6-ounce "co-cola", or a Frostie root beer. As you can imagine, that made Steak and Shake special.

Here's some of the things we did on a typical day at the beach. Rent a canvas float. This had to be done early. In July, the beach would be packed so if you didn't get one early you were out of luck. The rental fee was $3 per day. Raft rental accomplished; we rode the waves until lunch. A tip for the guys, if you rent a canvas raft to ride, always wear a t-shirt. The canvas on those rafts is rough as sandpaper. Combine that roughness with the salty water, and you get a bad case of raw nipples. Yes guys, wear a t-shirt. I almost forgot, before we hit the beach our mothers would slather us with Coppertone. Sunblock? We don't need no stinking sunblock. Besides, it hadn't been invented yet. I still love the smell of Coppertone, it was unmistakable. To me it screams beach. Some folks would describe it's smell as a blend of jasmine, rose, lavender, and lilac. Maybe, but I'd add the smell of the ocean and car exhaust to that list. The company's tanning lotions have changed formulas over the years, so they no longer smell the same. Sad really, nothing brings back memories of beach-time fun like the bright and happy smell of Coppertone.

Lunch was as described above, unless the dad's roasted hotdogs.

Before we hit the beach for the afternoon, we got another slather of Coppertone. By 1 o'clock it was H-O-T, and the humidity was thick enough to see. More wave riding, and then it was time to play in the sand. That was fun, but I sure hated getting sand in my crack. Sandcastle built, we hit the waves again, sandy crack problem solved. Out of the ocean by 4, that's when the rafts were returned. Next the pool, or as my dad called it "the warsh hole." I usually took a swim mask and flippers. Pool time for me was a *Sea Hunt* adventure, diving for pennies Dad tossed into the pool.

On the first day getting blistered was a requirement. Our mom's created all kinds of homemade treatments, but I think the most effective was dabbing room temperature tea on the skin. If that didn't work, you could always get a bottle of Solarcaine. If I got too sunburned, Dad would take me crabbing in the Halifax River. It was fun to catch them, but we threw them back. Crab was not something we knew how to cook, nor were we ready to try and eat it.

Elvis stayed just down the beach from us. At least that was the rumor. Supposedly, he loved the Copacabana Beach Motel on the corner of Silver Beach Boulevard and S. Atlantic Avenue. I suspect that was a marketing ploy by the motel. We never saw him, but the place was always full.

Daytona Beach was where I fell in love with seafood. We usually ate seafood a couple of times during the week. Anchors Inn was our favorite place. It was cheap, and the food was plentiful. I ate my first fried shrimp there.

B&B Seafood was a little more upscale. The first time I took my wife there was memorable. She was more country than me. Mom ordered us a boiled shrimp appetizer. I was noshing away when I heard her say, "These things sure are crunchy." I forgot to tell her to peel them. She was embarrassed, and I was too. We still laugh about that today. Sadly, both restaurants are long gone. There's a strip mall where Anchor's Inn sat. The site of B&B Seafood is just a bare, concrete slab.

I guess my fondest memory of Daytona Beach is the time spent there with Mom and Dad. Like I said earlier, they loved the beach, and instilled in me that same love. The last few years of their lives my wife and I took them to their happy place. When Dad became unsteady on his feet his wave riding days were over, and Mom couldn't get a tan anymore. As she got older sun exposure gave her sun poisoning.

These were still happy times. We'd haul a tent down to the beach. Once we got the chairs set up, we'd help Mom and Dad to the chairs. Always had a cooler filled with sandwiches, Cokes, and other snacks made for the day. All of us sat there staring dreamily at the ocean or chatting about people we saw walk by. Thongs were just coming into fashion. Dad chuckled and called them "butt floss." Mom talked about how uncomfortable they were. In the end, the roles were reversed, and that's OK. They took me to Daytona Beach for years. I only took them for a few, but I cherish those memories. Wait, I think I hear the ice cream truck. "Mom, Dad, can I have a quarter?" I wish…

JUDY'S HABANERO SHRIMP AND KILLER GRITS

My wife loves to cook. There are all kinds of Shrimp and Grits recipes out there. This is her variation on that theme. It really is "killer," and I love it. I hope you will too.

Ingredients

- 1 ½ cups chicken broth
- 1 ½ cups half and half
- 1 lime, juiced
- 4 tablespoons unsalted butter, cubed
- 1 teaspoon crushed red pepper
- 1 large Vidalia onion, chopped
- 1 cup uncooked stoneground, old-fashioned grits
- 1 cup shredded white cheddar cheese
- 5 thick-sliced bacon strips, chopped
- 1-pound uncooked shrimp (31-40 per pound), peeled and deveined

- 1 garlic clove, minced
- 1 ear fresh corn
- ½ cup water
- 3 green onions, chopped
- 1 Habanero pepper, finely chopped
- 2 tablespoons fresh parsley, chopped

Instructions

1. Place peeled and deveined shrimp into bowl, add lime juice, toss well, and set aside.
2. Cut corn kernels from cobb into bowl and set aside.
3. In a frying pan, cook bacon over medium heat. When done remove and set aside.
4. Remove 1 tablespoon of bacon drippings (grease), discard the rest, and place the tablespoon back into the frying pan. Set aside.
5. In a saucepan, over medium-high heat, melt 2 tablespoons of butter. Add the chopped garlic and sauté for 1 to 2 minutes. DO NOT let the garlic brown.
6. In the saucepan, add the half and half, chicken broth, and water. Bring to a low boil.
7. Add the reserved bacon, and corn kernels, green onions, and crushed red pepper, and grits.
8. Reduce heat and cook until the grits are done (15 to 20 minutes). Stir often and add water if necessary to attain your desired consistency.
9. Stir in the white cheddar cheese.
10. Place the frying pan with the bacon drippings (grease) over medium-high heat and add chopped Vidalia onions. Cook until clear, in fact they can be a little golden if you like.
11. Push the cooked onions to one side, add the finely chopped Habanero pepper and the shrimp and lime juice mixture and cook, stirring onions, peppers, and shrimp together until shrimp are pink, then

add parsley.

Serve shrimp mixture over girts and enjoy!

THE BEACH IN WINTER

I walked on the beach in winter.
The wind blew and the waves crashed on the sand.
The spray hit my face.
It felt like needles, and I turned away.
It was a lonely, wondrous place.

The gulls called out their hunter's cries.
They circled as best they could in winter's wind.
They dove for their food, splashed,
and rose again with their prize.
Their cries seemed to set my mood.

I found comfort in the roar of the surf.
The sound rose and fell like a woman's breasts as she sleeps.
Back and forth, in and out
went the sea on its endless journey.
It was beautiful. No doubt.

I got lost in my thoughts of you.
Like the surf they rose and fell and crashed in my mind.
Warming me like the winter sun above.
You are like the sea, beautiful, and I am in love.

AH YES, THE AUTOMOBILE

As you probably know by now, I'm a Southerner. That means different things to different people. The differences in opinion are usually, but not always, regional. The South is among many things, a car culture. We have little public transportation, and even littler use for it. Mainly because it doesn't go anywhere. Take Atlanta, please! Sorry Henny Youngman, I couldn't resist. In the 1970's, with much hoop-la, Atlanta opened its rapid rail system. When it opened it went nowhere near the Atlanta-Fulton County Stadium where the Braves and Falcons played. It didn't go to the airport. It didn't go past any of the major hospitals like Emory, Grady Memorial or Dekalb General. You get the idea. I admit some of those issues have been addressed in 2023, but Atlanta is still a car town. So is every other city south of the Mason-Dixon line. This phenomenon is not exclusive to the South. Cities like Los Angeles and San Diego, both on the west coast, are car towns. But car culture is as Southern as cornbread and buttermilk.

I learned to drive by myself in my dad's 1954 Chevy pick-up. That old truck had a clutch with 3-speed shifter on the column. Today you only get clutches and shifters in sports cars and big rigs. More about the perils of the clutch later. I got my learners permit in 1967. Most of the driving I did with my learners was in the family car. It was an automatic. That was easy. You only had to remember D to go forward and R to go backward and keep it between the lines. Also, lookout for trees, dogs, people, and the odd other driver. There was 1 redlight between home and Lawrenceville. No redlights between home and Lithonia. There weren't any between home and Stone Mountain either. Like I said, easy-peasy. The truck was another animal.

The day I got my license Dad took me out to the parking lot at Zoar. He switched off the truck, and we changed places. Remember, I'm 16 years old, and like most my age I considered myself a genius. I'd been driving for a year now. I had it down pat. This was nothing, I thought, as I turned the key. To my horror, and Dad's delight, the truck started bucking like a wild stallion. No, it didn't crank, but without the clutch engaged it was trying to move. I immediately killed the switch. Dad said, "You ain't as smart as you thought you were, are you?" "No sir," I sheepishly replied. "Are you ready to learn how to drive a stick now?", he said. "Yes sir," was all I could muster. Dad knew how to get my attention.

He patiently took me through how to do all the shifting as we sat there. I learned there are 2 ways to start a car with a clutch; in neutral with the parking brake and foot brake engaged, or with the shifter in 1st gear, with the parking and foot brakes engaged, and the clutch pressed in. Whew! That's a long sentence. Anyway, I finally started the truck using option 2. Dad said, "Let the clutch out." He forgot to add, slowly. A leap, a sputter, and she went dead. This was repeated several times until I got the hang of it. Finally, I was cruising around the parking lot in first gear. I was proud of myself, until Dad said, "Are you ever going to shift to 2nd?" Gee whiz, there was a whole lot more to this than I thought. Dad made it look easy, but it's not the first time. I won't bore you with the rest of the lesson. Suffice it to say, soon I was whizzing around Centerville like a pro.

Let me back up a little bit and tell you 2 stories about my pre-driving days. First story: Nicky Garner, his 56 Chevy, and a terrifying ride. We spent a lot of time with the Garners. Mom and Dad played Canasta with them, and we guys would hang out. One night we were at their house, and Nicky said, "Let's go for a ride." He had a souped-up 56 Chevy Bel-Aire. The car was turquoise and white, with a rolled and pleated interior. I think it had a 283 4-barrell engine. No matter, it was cool. I found out that night it would fly. We jumped in the car and headed toward U.S. 78. At the highway, we turned toward Stone Mountain. Richie wanted to get an ice cream so to the Dairy Queen we did go. They had curb service, so we ordered and started back toward Centerville. At the first redlight a couple of guys in a red 65 Mustang pulled beside Nicky and revved their motor. It was on. At the green light, Nicky and the Mustang guy took off burning rubber. We got the jump on him and took the lead. I was in the back seat, so I could see the speedometer. I began to hyperventilate when we hit 100mph.

We passed the turn for home at 110 m.p.h. It was late, so the traffic was light. I said, "Where we going?" Nicky replied, "Possum Lake." That was the old name of the lake. Development was just starting out our way, and the new name the developer choose was Lake Lucerne. When we got to "Possum Lucerne" Nicky downshifted, braked hard, and made the turn onto Lake Lucerne Road. We were on 2 wheels, I think. I can't be sure because I had my eyes closed tight, and my hands over my ears. I covered my ears because Richie was whooping and hollering when he wasn't laughing manically. The quick turn took the Mustang's driver by surprise, so we got a bit of a lead. We went through that subdivision flying. The only time I looked we were doing 80 m.p.h. The area was hilly so every time we topped a hill, we got some air. The Mustang finally gave up, thank the Lord. I was never so glad to be anywhere as I was to be back in the Garner's driveway. I never rode in a car with Nicky Garner again.

My best friend growing up was Gary Brownlee. We played many wiffleball major league games in his side yard. Gary was almost a year older than me, so he got his driver's license first. I'm not sure how he got it, but he got a car. A somewhat road weary 57 Chevy. He painted it himself with cans of spray paint. He choose flat black. He came over to the house on afternoon and asked me if I wanted to ride over to Keith Frachiseur's house. I asked Granny, and to my astonishment she said yes, so off we went. The astonishment at yes came from Granny's strictness. I was expecting no. However, she did say I had to be back home in an hour. Most of our roads around Centerville were dirt, including Sims Road where Keith lived. When we got on Sims Gary goosed it a couple of times to make it throw gravel. No problem. We arrived at Keith's and spent about 20 minutes shooting the breeze about nothing. As we left, Gary kicked it as he made a left on Sims. He held the pedal down a little too long. We fish-tailed a couple of times and slid right off the road and into the ditch. I almost soiled myself. We climbed out of the car and believe it or not there was no damage. Not even a scratch. Gary drove that old 57 right out of that ditch and delivered me back home safe and sound. I never rode in a car with Gary Brownlee again.

That brings me to my first car. After I got my license, I told my parents I needed a car. Did you get that? I needed a car! Dad said fine, we'll see about getting you one. My 16-year-old mind began to fantasize about the 1969 Plymouth Roadrunner they were going to buy me. It was Barracuda Orange and had a 383cu engine. Dad came home from work and said I found your car. So, we went to see my car. Somehow my Roadrunner had morphed into a silver 1964 Ford Falcon with a 140cu in-line 6 cylinder and 3-speed shifter on the column. The man wanted $400. I looked it over, and it wasn't bad. Dad told the man we'd take it, and we'd pick it up tomorrow. On the way home Dad asked how much money I had saved. I said about $450. He said great, you'll have some gas money left.

I started cutting grass when I was 10. The $450 came from that, and the work I'd done for Mr. Floyd Johnson. Dad said, "Son, you need to pay for that car yourself. Nothing is free in this old world so you might as well get used to that. Your mom and I will pay the insurance. You buy the gas and pay for maintenance." At 16 I thought that was tough, mean even. Looking back, I'm glad we did it that way. It was a good life lesson, and I think I'm better for it.

The first thing I did was head to Treasure Island to by an 8-track tape player. The Falcon had an AM radio, but who listened to AM? I choose an under dash mounted model with wedge speakers. I installed it myself. The first 8-track I bought was *Led Zeppelin II*. You know the one with *Ramble On* and *Whole Lotta Love*. The stereo on *Whole Lotta Love* was amazing. I had a car, a stereo, and gas was cheap. I was free, or so I thought.

In 1968 I started dating Judy Harrison. I met her at South Gwinnett High, and in the 10th grade I decided I was going to marry her. I did, in 1970. Our dating experiences in the old Falcon were memorable. Why? For all the times it failed to be reliable. It's embarrassing when you're parking in the back of a graveyard, and the car won't start. We were able to get it started by pushing it off. Another time it died in an inopportune place, and we caught a ride with a carload of drunks. Another time we were coming home from a movie in Tucker. The route took us down a dark, lonely road. At the darkest point on the road, old not-so-faithful decided it'd had enough. This was before cellphones. We had to walk down a long driveway, ring a stranger's doorbell, and ask to use their phone. This scenario happened several times. I always called Dad, and God bless him, he always came. He never complained, but he was like that. One Sunday morning, I was heading to pick Judy up for church, and the front end collapsed. A tie rod end just broke. It was always something.

After graduation in June of 1970 Judy and I decided, the Falcon had to go. I put a for sale sign on it and sold it for $400 in about a week. A local man bought it, and immediately painted it baby blue. I never understood that. The interior was red, and he kept it red. Earl Sheib must have had that baby blue paint on sale. Judy had some savings, and I did too. We pooled our money and bought a brand new 1970 VW Beetle. Her daddy threw a hissy fit because we weren't married. We didn't have any more breakdowns after that. Dad and Judy were relieved.

CENTERVILLE SCHOOL PEANUT BUTTER COOKIES

We had 2 great lunchroom ladies at Centerville School Mrs. Kate Johnson, and Mrs. Ophelia Campbell. They made all our meals from scratch. We had these cookies about twice a month. I found this recipe in my late mother's papers. I am blessed to have it and pleased to share it with you.

Ingredients

- 2 cups sugar
- 1/2 cup butter
- 1/2 cup Crisco
- 2 eggs
- 2-1/2 cups flour
- 1 cup peanut butter
- 1/4 tsp salt
- 1/2 tsp soda

Instructions

1. Preheat the oven to 375 degrees Fahrenheit.
2. Cream shortening and butter and sugar.
3. Add eggs. Beat.
4. Add peanut butter.
5. Mix flour, salt, soda and add to mixture.
6. Roll in ball then mash with fork.
7. Place in oven for 10 minutes, or until the edges are golden.
8. Cool on the baking sheets briefly before removing to a wire rack to cool completely.

Enjoy!

THE TRUTH ABOUT WAR

The sedan turned off Main and
slowly headed down the tree-lined street.

The house where hope once lived
was easy to find. Just look for the star.

Stopping at the walkway they sighed,
and the chaplain breathed a prayer.

Letter in hand, they walked in
full dress uniforms trying not to march.

The dreaded knock and the pregnant
silence gave birth to ashen faces.

Once more heartbroken cry's and
Silent pain met the soldiers at the door.

One more the long exhausting walk
Comes to an end with the same result.

Thanks ring hollow in the ears and
hearts of ones lost just inside the door.

About face, to the rear march, back
to the car, and on to the next one.

666,441 times in the last 250 years
rich men have lived, and poor men died.

Our fields, were not soaked in blood,

yet accepted their remains willingly.

Perhaps our tears prepared the soil
for we knew they were coming.

This is the truth about war.

GET ME ON A SOUTHBOUND TRAIN

I've always loved trains. When I was little, I could hear the whistles of the freight trains going through Stone Mountain. As I got older, I could hear the whistle of the tourist train in Stone Mountain Park. Sometimes, if the wind was right, I could hear both. This happened mostly at night in the summertime because I slept with the window open. The love of trains led to my love of songs about trains, and those who drove, rode, or were associated with them.

Songs sometimes use trains as metaphors. Others use railroads and trains as part of the story. For instance, the old Robert Johnson blues tune, *Love in Vain* from 1937. Its 3rd verse is the one I remember. It goes,

> "When the train, it left the station
> With two lights on behind
> When the train, it left the station
> With two lights on behind
> Well, the blue light was my blues
> And the red light was my mind
> All my loves in vain."

Yes, I know the Rolling Stones covered *Love in Vain* on their 1969 album *Let it Bleed*. I just prefer the original. There're also songs that recreate the clickity-clack sound of the wheels on the rails. Folklorist Howard Odum spent his life researching and recording African American music, folklore, and life. He often wrote about how black musicians could imitate train sounds. Railroads, trains, and those who work on, or ride them are fixed deep in our culture. And when it comes to songs, most of those are sung with a Southern accent.

Southerners, both black and white, have long loved railroads. This love blossomed, even though railroads were dangerous for passengers and workers. They allowed disease to spread much faster than wagons, horses, or walking. And who could forget outlaws like the James Gang. If those boys weren't robbing banks, they were robbing trains. It didn't take long for railroad companies to become dangerous too, but in a different way. By the last half of the 19th Century these companies were huge and able to impose their will on the American economy. As always, this hurt farmers, and small businesses. Suddenly, trains and railroads weren't so cool. It seems to me, that this love-hate relationship drove the rise of train lore and songs. Especially in the South, where storytelling is akin to breathing.

It's also more just than the impact of railroads on Southern history. The rise of Southern train songs parallels popular culture in America too. It mirrors, I think, the way the rest of the country sees the South, and the railroad. Railroads were once considered very modern. Not so much anymore, in fact trains and train travel now arouse a sense of nostalgia.

In thinking about train songs, and doing a little research, I came across and interesting book. It's not about trains, it's about how American popular culture "created" the South. The book was written by historian Karen Cox in 2013. It's called *Dreaming of Dixie: How the South was Created in American Popular Culture.* It's a tad academic. Nevertheless, Ms. Cox makes some good points. She states that non-Southerners created the false image of slowness and simpler days. This was due, she believes, to the turmoil of the first 30 years of the last century. Musicians and artists created myths about the old plantation life. The South became the land of "moonlight and magnolias." Songs about Dixie in this era were an escape. Audiences were transported to a safe, pre-industrial world. A fantasy world where plantations were romantic places. A place where the odor of honeysuckle and verbena filled the air. And of course, happy, singing slaves abounded. Those songs created and spread myths about our region. They, like all "Old South" and "Lost Cause" lore, ignored the horrors of slavery and its aftermath.

Today most Southern artists, and some others, take a more honest look at the injustices. Still, the image of the South as backward, slow-moving, and sometimes idyllic endures. Trains are part of that "down home" Southern image. They live in Nashville's pop-country fantasy world of pickups, "Daisy Dukes," ball caps, beer drinking, and country stores. And don't forget those good old, god-fearing small towns.

I propose a what if. What if Southern train songs veered from the fantasized Dixie. What if they turned from, no ran from, the sterile music that is modern country? Such train songs could point out the false South and help us get past that. The history of our region is complex. We all need to wrestle with that history to get at the truth.

Here are some of my favorite Southern train songs. They're in no particular order. Some are old, some are relatively new. They all, in different ways, examine our railroad history. These are my, purely subjective choices. This list is not meant to be exhaustive. I do think my Southern train songs look at the fluid impressions the South and railroads held and hold in the American psyche.

The Band – The Night They Drove Old Dixie Down - 1969

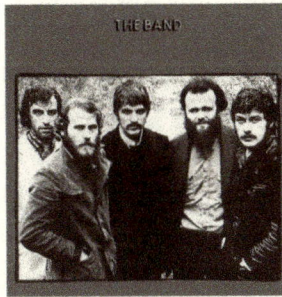

Virgil Caine is out of a job. Yankee calvary have torn up the tracks of the "Danville train." He's talking about the Richmond & Danville line. Southern railroads played a key role in the Civil War. The Confederacy used its rail network to move supplies and troops with great effect. This made their railroads targets for Union generals like Stoneman and Sherman. They destroyed the tracks, and burned the ties whenever and wherever they could. The song does flirt with the Lost Cause myth and focuses on the white Southern experience. While old Virgil was dejectedly walking home, African Americans were celebrating the arrival of Union troops, and the freedom they brought. Even so, Virgil's story shows the personal struggles of many Confederate veterans. Like most, Virgil turns his back on his lost railroad job and heads home to the land. After the war, railroads became even more essential to the South. By the 1880s, the Southern rail network doubled in mileage. Henry Grady, and these new railroad lines, helped create the image of a New South. A South rising like a Phoenix from the ashes.

Drive By Truckers – The Day John Henry Died – 2004

I'm sure most of you have heard the tragic story of John Henry. As historian Scott Nelson discovered, the real John Henry was an African American man from Virginia. He committed a minor crime and ended up in the convict labor system. John Henry's sentence was digging tunnels on the Chesapeake & Ohio Railroad. He died of silicosis; a lung disease brought on by breathing silica. John was buried in a nameless grave with dozens of others who died building this road. That's the real John Henry's story. It's not pretty and speaks to the terrible human cost of the South's rapid railroad growth after the Civil War. The legend of the John Henry we know shows how fast stories grew in the ever-moving work camps. As storytellers and singers retold the story it changed. They created a John Henry with super-human strength. A man who won a race with a machine. However, John Henry was a real man. His sad, true story doesn't change. The John Henry legend has changed often. The Drive-By Truckers version, written by a young Jason Isbell, is my favorite.

Vernon Dalhart – Wreck Of The Old 97 – 1924

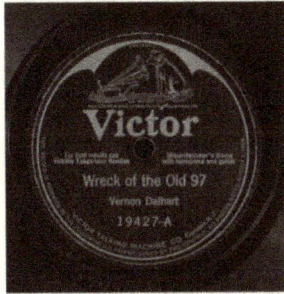

There's a direct connection between train-wreck songs and railroad expansion, especially in the South. These grisly story-songs spread rapidly as the wrecks piled up. By 1900, the pace of growth in the South, and the lack money, meant Southern railroads were dangerous. A lot more dangerous than anywhere else in the country. Is there any surprise that most train-wreck tunes are set in the South? The *Wreck of the Old 97*, is about a real derailment of a fast mail train. Oddly enough, the wreck happened outside Danville, Virginia (remember old Virgil Caine), in 1903. The song is a typical train-wreck ballad. Old Pete, the engineer, was late. He tried to make up lost time, and bad things happened. Some folks will tell you that this song is metaphorical. They say it's really about the South's struggle to transition from a farming economy to an industrial one. To this I say bull feathers! This is about a real wreck. Speed and lost time were the cause of many wrecks. Pete, the engineer, was "found in the wreck with his hand on the throttle, scalded to death with the steam." Sounds like what happened to Casey Jones and George Alley, both real people, who died when their engines wrecked.

Bessie Smith - Yellow Dog Blues - 1925

A lover leaving on a train is a popular, powerful theme. African Americans began leaving the South in increasing numbers during World War I. This migration spawned several songs like *Yellow Dog Blues*. Many of these old blues' songs were named after railroad companies. Lines like the Illinois Central or Louisville & Nashville got blamed for the heartbreak of those left alone in the South. *Yellow Dog Blues* is the just the reverse. Instead of South to North it goes North to South. Even so, the railroad still gets the blame. Poor Miss Susie Johnson's lover has left her. He's riding on "a southbound rattler besides the Pullman car." He got off "where the Southern cross 'the yellow dog." That's a real place. A junction in Moorhead, Mississippi. It's where the Southern Railway and the Yazoo Delta (Yellow Dog) Railroad met. W.C. Handy, the Father of the Blues, wrote the song in the 1910s. He recorded it several times but didn't release his version until 1922. His recording is a classic, but I prefer Bessie Smith's. She captures the sadness of this timeless blues tune.

Hank Snow – The Golden Rocket – 1950

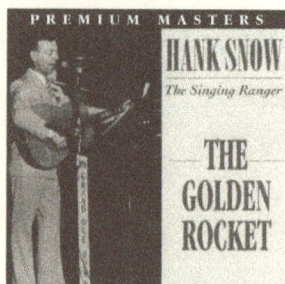

Now folks this here is a country train song. Hank Snow needs to "roll his blues away." He sees the way to do that is to ride south on the Golden Rocket. As I mentioned earlier, train travel lost its appeal in the late 19th century. It continued to decline into the early 20th century. The biggest reason in the early 20th century was the rise of cars. Henry Ford had made them affordable. Hey, he'd you sell any car you wanted if you'd take it in black. By the mid-20th century, railroad companies decided to fight back. They began building and promoting modern, sleek trains they called streamliners. It worked for a while, but ultimately failed. Eisenhower's interstate highway system drove the nail in the coffin. Ah, but for a moment these mid-century modern trains led to a railroad travel revival. The Golden Rocket streamliner train was never built. It existed only on paper. But no matter, Hank Snow tapped into that mid-century rail travel trend. He also added to the illusion of the romance of travel to the South. For Snow, the South is a place of escape, adventure, and reunion with his lover down in Tennessee. It was so joyous that the conductor bursts into song like a Broadway Show as the Golden Rocket crosses the Mason-Dixon Line. A brakeman even joins him. Reality was not the goal. Why have reality when fantasy will do? The song was released in 1950. The Civil Rights Movement was beginning to percolate. Things were far from the cheerful, pleasant South Snow wrote about. *The Golden Eagle* gives us a great example of how pop culture saw the South. It was still the "sunny old southland." A place far removed from the turmoil of the industrialized North.

Steve Goodman – City Of New Orleans - 1971

This train song is the train song of all train songs. First recorded by Steve Goodman in 1971, it's become one of those songs everyone wants to cover. And many did...Arlo Guthrie was the first in 1972. Willie Nelson took it to number one on the country charts. Goodman's English version has been covered by John Denver, The Seldom Scene, Johnny Cash, Jerry Reed, Judy Collins, and even David Hasselhoff. Canadian singer Roch Voisine recorded it in English and French. New Orleans songwriter, pianist and singer Allen Toussaint played it live in just about every show. He finally recorded his version live at the 2010 New Orleans Jazz and Heritage Festival. Now, about the train the song is about. The City of New Orleans train ran on the Illinois Central. It traveled between New Orleans and Chicago. This train has a lot of history. It saw everything from Civil War campaigns to Casey Jones's infamous wreck. It was one of many trains that took African Americans to the industrialized north. In *City of New Orleans* Goodman takes us on a "southbound odyssey" from Chicago. He wrote the song in 1970, amid declining passenger rail ridership. I see *City of New Orleans* as sort of a eulogy to train travel. Rail travel is dying, and that fact gives Goodman the "disappearing railroad blues." Images of nostalgia and decline fill the song. For instance, a car full of old men playing cards, and the views decaying buildings and "rusted old automobiles." Goodman gives a nod to the history of the train's importance to Southern African Americans too when he sings of "graveyards of old black men" and "sons of Pullman porters." As his City of New Orleans rolls "through the Mississippi darkness," Goodman takes us further south. Yes, further into and through a vanishing fantasy and into the past. "Good morning, America how are ya" indeed.

If you haven't heard this one in a while, go to your favorite music streaming service and give Steve Goodman's original recording a listen. It's a classic of the genre.

Gillian Welsh – Dawn Along The Dixie Line – 2011

Lastly, we come to Gillian Welch's *Dawn along the Dixie Line*. In this song, she takes the view of the Southerner stuck up North and missing the South. She uses Southern images and fast freight trains to tell the tale. Images like plucking banjos, ripe watermelons, and the ever present "river of whiskey." The song's dreamy tempo helps to conjure the slower pace of the Southern landscape, and of trains creeping along in the distance. Welsh, as many before her, draws us into a South that's out of space and out of time. The singer longs for the comfort of her Southern home, but the train's gone. The narrator mourns that "they pulled up the tracks now." She can never go back to the South she once knew. It's strange, I guess, but the railroad doesn't seem out of place in this fantasy. She longs for the "Dixie Line," and that brings us full circle. The two nostalgic pictures of the South and the train blend into one.

One final thought from the late, great Johnny Cash. Here's the chorus of his song *Come Along and Ride This Train*.

"Come along and ride this train
Come along and ride this train
Cross the mountains prairies reservations
Rivers levees plains
Come along and ride this train."

MOM 'S OLD-FASHIONED COCONUT PIE

Here's Mom's second go-to pie, and Dad's favorite; Coconut Cream Pie. I am very fond of this one too. When she took this to a reunion or church covered dish, folks would get a slice of this before the "real" food. If you waited until you finished the "real" food, you missed out.

Ingredients

Pie Crust:

- 1 1/4 cups all-purpose flour, plus more for dusting (see Mom's Note)
- 2 teaspoons granulated sugar
- 1/8 teaspoon fine salt
- 1 stick (8 tablespoons) cold unsalted butter, diced
- 1 large egg, lightly beaten

Mom's Note:

If you don't have your flour sifted, spoon it into a dry measuring cup and level off excess. Never compact your flour. Scooping directly from the bag compacts the flour and makes the crust dry.

Filling:
- 3 large egg yolks
- 1/4 cup cornstarch
- 1 cup whole milk
- 1 cup half-and-half
- 1/2 cup sugar
- 1/4 teaspoon kosher salt
- 2 tablespoons unsalted butter
- 1 teaspoon pure vanilla extract
- 1 cup sweetened shredded coconut

Meringue Topping:
- 3 large egg whites
- 1/4 teaspoon cream of tartar
- 6 tablespoons sugar
- Pinch kosher salt
- 1/2 teaspoon pure vanilla extract
- 1/3 cup unsweetened flaked coconut, toasted

Instructions

1. For the pie crust: Pulse the flour, sugar, and salt in a food processor fitted with the metal blade until combined. Add the butter and pulse until it resembles yellow cornmeal mixed with bean-size bits of butter, about 10 times. Add the egg and pulse 4 to 5 times until the dough forms a ball. (If the dough is very dry add up to a tablespoon more of cold water.)
2. Transfer the dough to a work surface. Form the dough into a disk, wrap with plastic wrap and refrigerate until thoroughly chilled, at least 1 hour.

3. Roll the dough on a lightly floured surface into a 12-inch circle about 1/8-inch thick. Transfer the dough to a 9-inch pie pan and trim the edges, leaving about an extra inch hanging over the edge. Tuck the overhanging dough underneath itself to form a thick edge that is even with the rim. Flute the edge as desired. Freeze the pie shell for 30 minutes.

4. Arrange a rack in the center of the oven and preheat to 400 degrees F. Put a piece of parchment paper or foil over the pie shell and fill with dried beans or pie weights. Bake on a baking sheet on the center rack until the dough is set, about 20 minutes. Remove from the oven and lift the sides of the parchment to remove the beans. Continue baking until the pie shell is lightly golden brown, about 10 more minutes. Cool on a wire rack.

5. For the filling: Whisk together the egg yolks, 1/4 cup of the milk and the cornstarch in a medium bowl until smooth and well combined. Stir together the remaining 3/4 cup milk, the half-and-half, sugar and kosher salt in a large saucepan. Heat over medium heat until barely simmering. Temper the egg yolks by slowly pouring the hot milk and cream into the egg yolks while continuing to whisk. Pour the custard back into the pan and place over medium-low heat. Cook, stirring constantly, until the custard is very thick and smooth, about 5 minutes; it will be the consistency of a pudding. (If the filling has scrambled a bit, or doesn't look smooth, strain it through a fine-mesh sieve into a separate bowl before adding the coconut.) Stir in the butter until melted, then stir in the vanilla and shredded coconut. Spread the filling into the cooled pie crust. Place plastic wrap directly on the surface of the pie and refrigerate until

chilled, about 2 hours, but preferably overnight.

6. For the meringue: Add the egg whites, sugar, cream of tartar and kosher salt to the bowl of a stand mixture fitted with the whisk attachment and whisk to combine. Place the bowl over a saucepan of simmering water, making sure the bottom of the bowl does not touch the water. Cook, whisking constantly, until the sugar dissolves and the mixture feels very hot to the touch. Transfer the bowl to the mixer and add the vanilla. Whisk on medium-high speed until stiff peaks form, 5 to 6 minutes.

7. Remove the plastic wrap from the pie and gently mound the meringue on top of the filling. Use an offset spatula to completely cover the filling and meet the crust all around the edges. (This will completely seal in the filling and help prevent weeping.) Use the offset spatula to form swirls and peaks in the meringue. Toast the meringue using a kitchen torch or broil in the oven until golden brown, keeping an eye on the meringue if broiling. Sprinkle all over with toasted coconut and serve.

NIGHT SKY

When I stare into the white speckled indigo of the night sky, I realize that I am nothing.

A mere microbe in the universe; Invisible to all except You and Your all-seeing eye.

Yet You, in Your immeasurable compassion, reached across the vastness of space to touch humanity.

A meteorite spins through the cold thin air leaving a trail of fire, and then it is gone.

It reminds me of You and Your short time here. Your fire left behind, unlike the meteorite's, doesn't fade.

The reality of You, and the fire that still burns brightly in those who belong to You is comforting.

The moon is a yellow-orange balloon setting the tops of the trees ablaze on the horizon.

It slowly creeps up into the night sky as if trying to be unnoticed by those of us watching.

Its brightness soon becomes a beacon to all who see it like Your words are to those who choose to hear them.

Let me be found among those who hear Your words and follow them as after life itself.

For as I stare into the white speckled indigo of the night sky, I realize that without You I am nothing.

COMING HOME TO ROCKY GROVE, AND THE RED-BACK HYMNAL

I know the title of this book is *Dust From a Red Dirt Road*, and memories abound within its pages. This story doesn't exactly follow the theme, but it's a memory, and it matters to me. So, here it is...

In 2012 we moved to paradise. It's also known as Tiger, Georgia. For 5 glorious years we lived in the northeast Georgia mountains. What a blessing it was. We were even more blessed, if that's possible, by the little country church we found. Rocky Grove Baptist Church took us in and loved us. They treated us like family, and that's the way church is supposed to be. Today the term "doing church" is popular. Let me tell you, there's a difference between "doing church" and being the Church. Rocky Grove is being the Church.

We'd been going to Rabun County for years. The two-lane road was familiar. It's a beautiful drive in the fall heading west toward Lake Burton. Late in the evening, the sun slowly setting on the horizon against the backdrop of a pink Georgia sky. We'd driven past Rocky Grove numerous times. Often, we'd comment about that "pretty little white church" on Bridge Creek Road. We never dreamed it would one day be our church home. Judy went first. She came home and told me she felt like she was home. I couldn't wait until next Sunday. We weren't Baptists, though Judy had grown up as one. I grew up Methodist but was Saved in a Baptist church. But we weren't Baptists. We'd spent the last, many years in Pentecostal churches. There weren't any churches of that flavor nearby, and Rocky Grove was right across the street from our house. I thank God for that. His providence is much better than our planning.

RGBC 1913 - 2000

Here's a brief history of the church. Rocky Grove is not a new church plant. It began as a Brush Arbor meeting sometime after 1825 on land owned by a Mr. David McClain. The church was charted in 1836 and began holding services in Mr. McClain's blacksmith shop. In January 1836 William Andrew Watts married Sara Jones, and they set up housekeeping in what was then called the Bridge Creek Community. Soon after their marriage William was ordained a minister. He, James Ellard, and James Jarrad took turns preaching. The church eventually built a building and worshiped in it until 1900. The land where Rocky Grove sits now was acquired in 1900, and a 24-foot by 11-foot building was built. It served as a both school and church until 1913. In that year, the church enlarged the 1900 building, and it stood until 2000, when the current building was built. The church's records before 1890 have been lost to time. Thus, very little is known about day-to-day goings on. We do know that prior to 1890, preachers, deacons, and lay members were named to preach the sermon when the church met. Oh, and they only met once a month.

RGBC Today

When next Sunday arrived, it was misting rain, so we drove the 500 feet to the church. We entered the parking lot and pulled into a space between two big trucks. Our Prius looked like a toddler standing between two lumberjacks. The lot was almost full. It was a little before 11. Yes, we overslept and missed Sunday School. The white clapboard church stands on a hill and was even prettier in the rain. It was January, so the trees in the churchyard were bare and pointing their boney fingers at the overcast sky. We got out of the car and headed inside.

The first person we met was the Pastor, Kyle Watts. He was very welcoming, but what I noticed right away was his eyes. I've never looked into Jesus' eyes, but looking into Pastor's would have to be similar. The love of Jesus seemed to flow from them. His handshake was firm. I was impressed. We nodded hello to others who were there, and they acted like they knew us. They crowded around shaking hands and introducing themselves. Let's see, we met Mark and Patti Brown, Jerry Burrell, Billy Carter, Barry Wood, and Phyllis Henderson. We've been to a lot of churches, but we've never been greeted like we were at Rocky Grove. As we entered the sanctuary, I thought it couldn't be better. I was wrong. Our neighbor, Kitty Cantrell, saw us, stood up, and said, "Howdy neighbor!' She knew us because she'd brought us a homemade cherry pie earlier in the week and invited us to church. I felt a tap on my shoulder, turned around, and met Max Watts. Brother Max was Pastor's father, and the patriarch of the church. I've only met one other man that impacted my life like Max would. His name was Lester Bearden. Both men were full of Godly wisdom. Lester was quiet, but when he spoke his words demanded attention. Max was an eloquent speaker, and a brilliant historian. The people were great, the service was powerful, and the singing, oh what singing. To my surprise, the hymnal was very familiar. It was the old, Church of God, Red Back Hymnal.

Now more about that Red Back hymnal. The actual name of the Red Back hymnal is "The Church Hymnal." It was found in pews of many denominations from the 1950s through the early 1970s. It was one of the first hard-back hymnals published. You see, most song books (hymnals) were paperback, and spiral bound. They weren't meant to be permanent. They were usually issued in series, and the publishers wanted you to buy the latest edition.

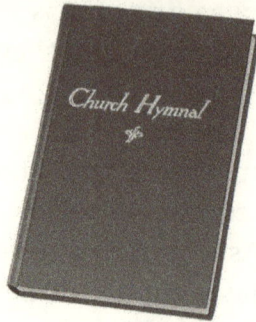

The publisher of "The Church Hymnal" was Tennessee Music and Printing Company, and it came off the press in November 1951. TMPC is the publishing division of the Church of God of Cleveland, Tennessee. What made it unique was its hard back, and its collection of popular hymns, old-time gospel favorites and songs to celebrate church holidays. All in one collection, in a book that would last. Oh, by the way, it's a shape note song book. If you don't know what that is, look it up. Or, better yet, go to YouTube and listen to some shape note singing. It's the sound of Heaven.

We sat with Kitty. I'd never been to Rocky Grove, so I wasn't sure exactly what to expect. Judy, however, was an old pro. After the announcements the song caller, Brother Max Watts, kicked us off with *Blessed Assurance*. Next came Heavens national anthem, *Amazing Grace*, then *Higher Ground*, and *At Calvary*. During the offering we sang the best country Gospel song ever written, *I'll Fly Away*. Judy and I didn't sing on key, and our pitch went from sharp to flat, but we enjoyed it anyway. We tapped our feet with the best of them, kept good time, and made a joyful noise. We connected with those around us, and with of our ancestors, who'd sung these same songs over the past few hundred years.

I know I keep talking about Max Watts, but I can't help myself. He was an amazing man. Brother Max knew ancient history, quoted the Bible flawlessly in conversation, and had a great memory. Instead of a special song or solo before preaching Max stepped up to the pulpit and delivered a recitation. The poem that day was *The Church Walking with the World* written by Matilda C. Edwards in 1936. The poem has 26 stanzas, 104 lines, and 759 words, and he never missed a word. It was impressive, and inspiring. When Max finished, Pastor Kyle entered the stand. He delivered a message straight out of the Bible. Imagine that. No shenanigans, or silly stories or jokes, just a passion for souls I hadn't seen in years. The man preached with tears running down his face. When the altar call was given folks came down to pray. The message was simple, powerful, and clear. After service, he stood at the back of the church shaking hands, hugging necks, and slipping candy to the children.

As we climbed back into the Prius, I looked at Judy and said, "You were right Babe, we're home." We'd been moved by the service, the presence of God, and the people. And the blessed songs in that old Red Backed Hymnal.

Footnote: We lost Max in 2022. Here's the obituary I wrote to mark his passing.

Max Welton Watts, 1935 - 2022

Have you ever moved? I mean really moved. Say a hundred miles or more away from home. I have. A long way from home and the property that's been in my family since 1924. Up into the beautiful NE Georgia mountains. Out in the country on a road called Bridge Creek.

Almost directly across the road from our cabin was a little white church. Rocky Grove Baptist Church it's called. Judy was the first to visit. She came in the door saying I think I've found us a church. I went next Sunday. She was right.

One of the first people I met was Brother Max Watts. He greeted me in the aisle, introduced himself, and shook my hand. It was like he'd known me all my life.

We settled into the rhythms of Church at Rocky Grove, and soon became members. I can honestly say I've never been around a more loving bunch of folks. And a lot of that loving attitude started with Max Watts.

He was not a highly educated man, as far as 'book learning' goes, but he was one of the most intelligent people I've ever known...a renaissance man for sure. Max could and did quote long poems from memory. My favorite was *The Church Walking with The World*. He was a historian, both ancient and modern and was fluent in discussing either or both. He was a genealogist and loved nothing more than researching and talking about his family. He was a theologian, a real Bible scholar. I loved to listen to him talk about the Book that he loved. Max was also a sage, full of Godly wisdom. When he spoke, you'd better listen, or you'd probably miss something you needed to know.

Brother Max left the bounds of this mortal sphere Wednesday, December 14, 2022. He was surrounded by his loving family as he stepped over the threshold and fell into the arms of Jesus. As it says in Revelation 21:4, "And God shall wipe away all tears from their eyes; and there shall be no more death, neither sorrow, nor crying, neither shall there be any more pain: for the former things are passed away." Max had the hope of Glory. Now he dwells in its reality.

Dear friends and family, especially Mrs. Edith, I pray for peace and comfort during this time of grief.I am beyond blessed to have known this precious man. This is just a temporary separation my friend. One day soon I'll know what you know now. Until that great day enjoy your reward.

Terry R. Freeman, 12/16/22

TERRY'S THUNDER SOUP (BLACK BEAN CHILI)

My take on chili. It's good...
Don't eat 3 days before you're going to be in an enclosed space. You know, like an airplane, car, train, spacecraft, or submersible. Not recommended for submariners, pilots, astronauts on space walks, or prisoners in solitary confinement.

Ingredients
- 1 lb lean (at least 80%) ground beef
- 1 large onion, chopped (1 cup)
- 1 large bell pepper (color of choice), chopped (1 cup)
- 2 cloves garlic, crushed
- 1 1/2 tablespoon chili powder
- ½ teaspoon salt
- 1 teaspoon red pepper flakes
- 1 teaspoon unsweetened baking cocoa
- ½ teaspoon red pepper sauce
- 2 cups diced tomatoes (from 28-oz can), undrained

- 1 can (19 oz) Progresso™ black beans, undrained

Instructions

1. In 3-quart saucepan, cook beef and onion over medium-high heat about 8 minutes, add garlic last 2 minutes, stirring occasionally, until beef is brown; drain.

2. Stir in remaining ingredients except beans. Heat to boiling. Reduce heat to low; cover and simmer 1 hour, stirring occasionally.

3. Stir in beans. Heat to boiling. Reduce heat to low; simmer uncovered about 20 minutes, stirring occasionally, until desired thickness.

Serve with a dollop of sour cream and/or grated cheddar cheese.

SUMMER THOUGHTS

I often walked alone on red dirt country roads.
Basking in the feel and smell of the sweet honeysuckle wind.
The hot sun blistered my back, and the tops of my feet.
The dust I kicked up drifted off through the pines.
Summertime in Georgia.
Blissful days of my youth.

Lazing on the banks of Yellow River; cane pole in hand.
The worms squirming in my fingers
in their futile attempt to avoid my Eagle Claw.
Catfish, Bluegill, and the occasional Yellow Perch.
Long, satisfying drinks of the cool river's water.
Peeing in the bushes near the falls.
I often wander back there in my mind.
My summer thoughts convince me that flowing
streams and lazy dreams are real.
It's life that's the illusion.

THE GREAT MAYONNAISE WAR

In Matthew's book Jesus talks about the end of days. Among other things He says we'll hear of wars and rumors of wars. That appears to be happening right before our eyes. Just look at the turmoil in this old world. That being said, have you heard about the great Mayonnaise War? Well, it's a thing so prepare yourselves. And hold onto to your "mater sammiches".

Speaking of tomato sandwiches…

There's nothing better than a tomato sandwich in the summertime. Made with untoasted, soft white bread, salt and pepper, a generous slathering of Blue Plate mayonnaise, and a tomato fresh from the vine sliced thick. I'm sure, after much study and prayerful consideration, that this is the meal served at the Marriage Supper of the Lamb. A variation of the tomato sandwich is the BLT, bacon lettuce and tomato sandwich. Exactly as described above except toast the white bread and add the bacon and lettuce. This is also quite popular. The great Southern institution, Waffle House, serves an excellent BLT.

Did you notice I said Blue Plate mayonnaise? I come from a Blue Plate family. For me, it's always been, and it'll always be Blue Plate. It's as Southern as fried pies and bacon drippings. Blue Plate was born in New Orleans in 1927. The brand took inspiration from blue "Willow Ware" plates, my mother's tableware of choice. Blue Plate is a symbol of home, family, tradition, and the good life. The simple recipe of oil, vinegar and egg yolks is heavenly. Blue Plate is an extra rich and creamy mayonnaise that tastes like homemade. One of the greatest publications in the world, *Southern Living* magazine, says this about the iconic condiment, "The legendary spread of the South deserves a pedestal in your kitchen." Though the earth give way, and the mountains fall into the heart of the sea, though its waters roar and foam, and the mountains quake with their surging (okay, I borrowed that from my favorite Psalm, number 46), my allegiance will remain with Blue Plate.

There are other, lesser brands out there. My first exposure to this fact was in high school. It was in the lunchroom at South Gwinnett High, home of the Comets, when the culinary earthquake occurred. We were talking about tomato sandwiches. This led to a discussion of the proper condiment. I was shocked and dismayed to hear other brands mentioned. Lesser mayonnaise pretenders, like Kraft, "Miracle" Whip (a misnomer if there ever was one), Duke's, and Hellmann's (the name says it all). I never imagined that any of those could mount a challenge to Blue Plate. Apparently, some of my friends weren't raised as well as I was.

In a poor attempt to be fair, let's look at the imposters, I mean other brands.

I'll start with Duke's. I thought Duke's was strictly a South Carolina thing, like red dots on liquor stores. I guess that's due to its history. During World War I, Eugenia Duke sold sandwiches to soldiers at Camp Sevier near Greenville, South Carolina. She made them with her homemade mayonnaise. Soldiers wrote to her asking for the recipe. Then a local store began selling jars her mayonnaise. The day she sold her 11,000th jar, Eugenia finally invested in a delivery truck. I would consider Duke's if I was on a desert island and that's all I had. It also has some merit because it was created in the South.

That brings us to the vastly inferior spreads. Kraft and Hellmann's, originating in Chicago and San Francisco, respectively. Need I say more? I hesitate to even mention Miracle Whip. I'm not sure what Miracle Whip is. That reminds me of a story.

A friend's mother, who shall remain nameless, made us ham sandwiches, once. There's a holy trinity of sandwiches in the South. Tomato, banana, and the ham sandwich. There's nothing more sacred to a Southern boy, than this trio. In order of reverence, the holy tomato sandwich, then the ham sandwich. Especially one made with smoked Virginia ham. Lastly the banana sandwich. All three require mayonnaise. When my friend's mother assembled the ham sandwiches, she covered the bread with three inches of white miracle slop. Then had the audacity to attempt to pass them off as food.

My cousin, Randy, took one bite and started to cry.

"What's wrong?" said my friend.

"Your mom uses Miracle Whip," said Randy.

"So?"

"So, I'm sure going to miss your mama when we're all up in heaven."

Now for Hellman's. I know a lot of people who use Hellmann's. And believe me, I'm not here to pass judgement. But surely their tastebuds are smoking crack. My aunt, for instance, uses Hellmann's for her deviled eggs. I once asked why, knowing that she too came from a Blue Plate home. She said, "Anything that's been deviled needs a little Hell." Then she laughed and licked a white glob of the automotive grease from her finger.

I once conducted an experiment hoping to settle the argument. I enlisted my friend, Rich, and his wife, Sandra to help. I knew they had a serious Hellman's habit. Rich and

Sandra brought along their son, Teddy. Teddy's nine years old. He spent most of the experiment bored senseless and digging in his drawers. Also, my wife joined us.

We all did a blind taste test in our dining room. My mother prepared several mayonnaise heavy recipes using Blue Plate, Duke's Hellman's, and Miracle Whip. She placed the food samples on the table. The five of us got busy.

First, we had deviled eggs. We sampled each one and wrote our score on slips of paper. Then came pear salad. Let me take a moment to explain. Some of you never had the privilege of eating lunch five-days-a-week in a Southern, public-school lunchroom. Pear salad was indispensable in the Southern lunchroom lady's menu rotation. Mrs. Campbell and Mrs. Johnson, our dear lunchroom ladies at Centerville School, served pear salad at least once a week. So, let me describe pear salad for you. It's a canned half pear with six cups of mayonnaise dolloped in the center. That's topped with a hand full of cheese. Oh, the glory of the memory floods me with emotion, and throws my saliva glands into overdrive.

After that came potato salad, the litmus test for mayonnaise.

When we finished our experiment, we folded our paper slips and placed them in a hat. It took two seconds to tally votes. And do you know what we found? Drumroll please. Every single person in the room unknowingly voted for...

Blue Plate mayonnaise.

A close second was Duke's. This didn't surprise me. I'm not from a Duke's family, but it's a good, old Southern brand.

Third place went to a jar of Vaseline.

Fourteenth place went to Hellmann's.

Miracle Whip got one vote. And I don't want to point fingers, but whoever voted for it spelled it wrong. That makes me think it was a nine-year-old. One named Teddy, who is a known Elmer's Glue eater.

Nobody touched the deviled eggs made with Miracle Whip. They had already burned a hole through the table and were glowing neon green.

So, I hope this highly unscientific experiment clears things up. I also hope that anyone out who disagrees with my findings remembers that because we disagree, doesn't mean that you're not completely insane. Now if you'll excuse me, I need to take this jar of Hellman's and go lubricate the axle on my truck.

CENTERVILLE LUNCHROOM PEAR SALAD

Our lunchroom ladies were wonderful. For my first 8 years of school, they made my lunch 5 days a week. One of my favorite dishes was pear salad. It's simple, made with pears, grated cheese, and mayonnaise. You can serve it as an appetizer or side dish with almost any meal.

Ingredients

- 3 cans Bartlett pears in water
- ¼ cup mayonnaise
- ½ cup grated Cheddar cheese
- 12 maraschino cherries

Instructions

1. Drain pears. Line platter with lettuce leaves or use a deviled egg platter and set pears out on dish.
2. Drop a dollop of mayonnaise in the center of each

pear, about a teaspoon or slightly more.

3. Place a large pinch of grated cheese on top of the mayonnaise. Garnish with a maraschino cherry. Serve pears chilled.

REMNANTS OF THE DAY

I relish the remnants of the day.
Late in the evening when the sun is low,
and shadows grow long.
Recollections of the past come my way.
They drift by ever so slowly,
though not all good, they're never wrong.

I'm warmed by the memories passing.
Strangely warmed by the fires they rekindle.
Like a beggar who finds a blanket on a cold night
I cling to the joy they bring.
As the light from the setting sun begins to dwindle.
Soon it's gone, as they are, but all is right.

For I savor the remnants of the day.
Everyday.

OCTOBER 1952

The years 1951 and 1952 have been called America's "Winter of Discontent." The people were frustrated by the standoff that was the Korean War. There appeared to be no end in sight. On top of that, the highly unpopular President Harry Truman wouldn't commit to seeking another term. Poor Truman felt that he had no chance to win after firing the highly popular General Douglas MacArthur.

Out of this turmoil came the "Draft Eisenhower Movement." It was the first successful political draft of the 20th century. The movement would take a private citizen to the White House. The popular WWII general, Dwight D. Eisenhower was talked into running for President. Both parties wanted him for his name and reputation. He eventually chose the Republican Party and was nominated. He beat the Democrat Party candidate, Adlai Stevenson, in the general election in November 1952. But I digress.

On January 2, 1951, 13 young men gathered at "The Drug Store" in Snellville. There wasn't a pharmacist on duty, so it wasn't really a drug store. They did stock a bunch of over-the-counter medicine, so the locals called it the drug store. They also had a soda fountain, and sold sandwiches, chips, and such. It was a gathering place that everyone knew. So, what was unusual about this gathering? There was a military recruiter involved. You see, the guys were considering joining up, even with the Korean War raging some 7,143 miles to the west. Folks thought the boys were very patriotic, and some probably were. However, as their sons would do 15 years later, most were avoiding the draft. Just like during the Vietnam War, most draftees went straight to the Army, and then to Korea. Sadly, for 36,914 young men the Korea trip was one-way.

The Snellville "13"*

Snellville was a small town in 1951. Its population in the 1950 census was a whopping 309. Gwinnett County only had 32,320 people, so Snellville had .01% of that population. Wow. As in any small town, word spread quickly about the gathering at The Drug Store. Before long, all the drug store cowboys, and other interested folks began showing up. They came for 3 reasons, to cheer them on, to warn them about what they were getting in to, or just to watch. At the end of the day, 11 men joined the Air Force, and 2 joined the Navy. They were called "The Snellville 13." My Dad was one of the Air Force 11. Apparently, not one to waste time, the recruiter arranged for a bus to pick up the Air Force boys the next day. Dad had few hours to say goodbye to Papa and Granny, and my soon to be Mom. On January 3, 1951, he boarded the bus to Atlanta, signed his official papers, and headed to basic training at Lackland Air Force Base in San Antonio, Texas.

Mom and Dad married on July 4, 1951. Dad was home on leave after basic training. They had a brief honeymoon of 48 hours. Then they jumped into Dad's yellow, 1940 Ford Coupe and headed up U. S. 78 to Memphis. The base at the Memphis airport was to be Dad's duty station for the next 3 and one-half years, or so they thought. They settled into a rented room near the base and began their married life.

I was conceived in Memphis, Tennessee right before Dad received his hardship discharge from the Air Force. Papa Freeman had a heart attack, and Dad being the only boy had to come home to tend to the farm. He received his DD-214 on February 22, 1952. He served one year, one month, and 18 days.

It was a cool 49 degrees, at 3:00A.M. the morning October 23' 1952, when Mom's water broke. She was 20 years old; Dad was 22. To say they were nervous and scared would be an understatement. Excited and terrified would be more accurate. They had a plan, and Dad put it into motion. He called his sister, Jeanette Gresham. Her job was to go with them to Georgia Baptist Hospital and keep Mom calm on the way. He called Daddy Bob and Nanny Pat so they could meet them there. Papa and Granny would keep the home fires burning. As soon as Aunt Jeanette arrived, they got Mom into that old 40 Ford, and took off for Atlanta. Mom said she laughed, cried, and hollered all the way. Aunt Jeanette held her hand, and Dad drove. He said he cried all the way too.

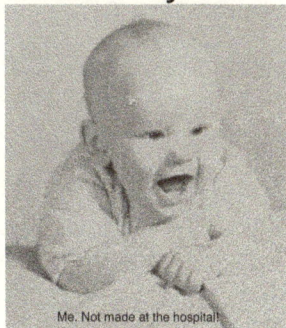

Me. Not made at the hospital!

I wish I could tell you I came right after they arrived, but I can't. I was warm and comfortable where I was, and in no hurry to make my appearance. Dad, Daddy Bob, Nanny Pat, and Aunt Jeanette settled in for what was to be a grueling 19 hour wait. Yes, my poor Mom had a difficult, scary labor. Dad said Daddy Bob didn't sit down the entire time. He just paced back and forth, praying, and wringing his hands. I finally arrived at 11:37 P.M. Dad burst into tears, and Daddy Bob began to whoop it up, shake everybody's hand, and pass out cigars. Nanny Pat and Aunt Jeanette were tired and happy. Aunt Jeanette said a lady in the waiting room told her she had never seen such a proud daddy. My aunt told her, "That ain't the daddy. That's the grandpa, and this is his first grandchild."

Like I said, the labor was rough. Mom couldn't see me until the late morning of the 24th. Dad had gone back to work. There wasn't any Family Medical Leave in those days. Mom and I were in the hospital for 2 weeks. We came home the morning of November 7, 1952. Georgia Power did let Dad off for the day so he could bring Mom and I home. Granny Freeman got everything ready, and Dad and Aunt Jeanette came to Atlanta to get us. Mom was still weak, so Aunt Jeanette held me on the way home. When we crossed the old one-lane Annistown Bridge Mom told me that Aunt Jeanette said, "You hear them boards clacking Terry? You know what that means? It means you're almost home." Papa and Granny were sitting on the porch waiting. Granny Freeman carried me into the house and placed me in my cradle. I was home.

I'm thankful that I interviewed Mom, Dad, and Aunt Jeanette. They're all gone now. In fact, sadly, everyone in this story is gone except me. My time will come soon enough. I live in the belief that this has been nothing but a brief separation. Yes, I believe that when I cross over to that golden shore, they'll be there waiting for me. What a glad reunion that will be.

*I'm forever grateful to Thomas "Pap" Ewing for the background information about the Snellville "13." Pap was one of those men. His article, "A Baker's Dozen From Snellville - 1951" appeared in the December, 2022 Snellville Historical Society Newsletter (Volume 22 Issue 3). Pap, thanks for your time, and breakfast at the Waffle House.

MOM'S CREAMED CORN

This dish is best prepared in a cast-iron skillet. We always used a variety called Trucker's Favorite. It's a white, mule corn, nowadays mostly used in animal feed. It's the best. Period. If you can't get mule corn, any old white corn will do. It ain't summer without creamed corn.

Ingredients

- 12 Ears of Corn
- 3 Tablespoons Butter
- 2 Tablespoons Flour
- 1 teaspoon Sugar
- Salt and Pepper to taste

Instructions

1. Remove shucks, clean, and silk the corn as needed.
2. Stand ear of corn on end inside a large bowl.
3. Cut halfway through the kernels of corn, slicing off with a sharp knife.
4. Using the back of knife, scrape out the remaining corn from each ear of corn.
5. Place butter in a skillet, over medium heat on your

stove top.
6. Add corn.
7. Add sugar.
8. Add Salt.
9. Add Black Pepper, to taste.
10. Stir and let cook until corn tastes done.
11. Mix 2 Tablespoons flour with 2 Tablespoons of water.
12. Pour flour-water mixture into corn.
13. Let cook for several minutes, until mixture thickens.

Serve warm and enjoy! It goes great with any summer vegetable. Field peas, butter beans, fried okra, or anything else you like. However, always serve with a sliced tomato, fresh out of the garden. Oh, and homemade biscuits.

Note:

If fresh corn ain't available, you can make this with frozen corn, or even canned corn. You'll need to mash up about half of the corn, to get the "cream" out of some of the kernels.

I'M GETTING OLDER

I think about death now.
I didn't used to.
I believed death would never make me bow.
Didn't old folks have anything better to do
than read the obits in the newspaper?

My thoughts of death don't make sense.
But I admit that they cross my mind.
You see, I'm not that dense,
but as I get older, I feel a little behind
if I don't check them out myself.

You never know.
I see people my age in there all the time.
I know I'm ready when it's my time to go,
but if it's OK with you I'll climb a later climb.
Jacob's Ladder is usually a one-way trip.

ZOAR CHURCH ROAD, CENTERVILLE COMMUNITY, GWINNETT COUNTY GEORGIA

As I'm sure you know by now, I come from Centerville Community, Gwinnett County, Georgia. The road, Zoar Church Road, in front of the house where I grew up was dirt. Red dirt. Some would call it red clay. It was just dirt to us. As hard as Stone Mountain granite when dry. Rain made it as sticky and slick as Vaseline on a doorknob. If you don't believe me there are plenty of facts in the historical record to back me up. I'll just mention a couple. Review the records of the Military Division of the Mississippi (Sherman) or the Army of Tennessee (Johnston). Both armies had problems with that red dirt in the spring and summer of 1864.

My paternal grandparents always lived with us in our home. Mom and Dad both worked at public work in the big city of Atlanta. Mom worked for Continental Insurance. Dad worked for Georgia Power. Their days started early and ended late. Granny and Papa Freeman got me up, fed, and off to school. They were there when I got home. I can still see them rocking on the front porch as the bus pulled up in the afternoon.

Usually there were some old-fashioned teacakes and a cold glass of milk waiting for me on the kitchen counter. I wore size "husky" as a boy. Any wonder why?

Granny Freeman never worked outside the home. She kept house and cooked. Boy could that lady cook. Her biscuits were heavenly. Papa used to say, "If you set one of Maude's biscuits up on yo fore hed yo tongue wood slap yo brains out tryin' to git it!" I never tried that, but Papa was a man of his word, so I know it's true. We ate her biscuits plain, with butter, with butter toasted, with butter and cheese toasted, with homemade jellies, jams, and preserves, with an egg, with farm-made sausage, with farm cured country ham, with farm cured bacon, with streak-o-lean, and as a side with every meal. When the biscuits got stale, which was rarely, Granny made bread pudding. All the vegetables were cooked in bacon grease or better yet with salt-pork, or fatback. What is salt-pork or fat back, you may ask? Salt-pork or fatback is as it sounds, the fat from the back of a pig. It is "hard fat" that can be chopped and ground. Salt-pork or fatback is salted and cured to prolong its shelf life. It is used in Southern cooking. It adds flavor and juiciness to greens, and other dishes. Salt-pork or fatback was also a standard provision in larders into the 20th century. Cooks like Granny Freeman used it because was relatively cheap and farm-made, it kept well, added flavor to meals, and provided an easily portable cooking fat. All vegetables got a fair dose of the stuff. I guess today we'd call her style soul food or Southern style. We just called it 'good eatin."

In the dry hot "dog days" of summer Zoar Church Road was dusty, real dusty. A puff of wind and the dust rose like a light orange fog. When it settled it covered everything inside and outside the house. A passing automobile had the same effect. We had no air conditioning, so the windows and doors were open in the summertime. That fine red dust went through the screens like they weren't even there. Granny dusted and swept every day just to stay ahead of the stuff. It was a losing battle, but she couldn't stand the thought of red dust in her biscuit dough.

Zoar Methodist Church (well, that is what it was when I was young) is the namesake of the road. The church sits about 100 yards east of the home place. Supposedly, Zoar was founded in 181. If that's true, the church was constituted before the county of Gwinnett was created. That happened in 1818 when the State of Georgia, complicit with the United States, stole some of it from the Cherokee and Creek Nations. The Cherokees had forced the Muscogee (Creek) off the land in the Northern part of what became Gwinnett County in the mid 1700's. My people, or most of the recent ones at least, lie at rest in the cemetery at Zoar. I come from a long line of Methodists. I still have trouble putting he word "United" in front of Methodist. Zoar has grown some, but it's still a little, white-clapboarded church. It used to stay a reddish pink until it rained. The tombstones across the road also stayed covered in the red dust.

We had a large elm tree in the front yard of the home place. It no longer stands. It finally succumbed to old age and blight. Mr. Brady planted it when he built the house sometime between 1890 and 1900, I think. By the time Papa, Nathaniel S. Freeman, bought the house and farm it was a good-sized tree. When I was small the tree seemed like a Giant Sequoia. It became a place to play with my cousin Wanda. We'd play with our toy cars between the roots. We had many Daytona 500 races around that old tree on our bicycles.

We rarely saw a car and when we did someone we knew was behind the wheel. They always went slow. I'm not sure if it was to keep from smothering us in dust, or because an old gravel road can be dangerous. The occupants would look toward the house. If someone was in the yard they would, as we say, "throw up their hand" and wave. A wave was not optional. To not wave was uppity. No one wanted to be uppity in 1961 so they'd wave, and we'd wave back. I often wondered if a stranger would wave. Maybe. Probably. Most people were friendly then.

Everyone who lived on Zoar Church Road was kin. I mean everyone. The most distant relation was a 1st cousin. We were all Freemans or issue of Freemans. It wasn't until much later in the 1960's that non-kinfolk started moving in on us. It was a happy life before that. Not a care in the world. Safe. That was Zoar Church Road when I was a boy.

MOM'S LEMON POUND CAKE

My Mom loved anything lemony. Lemon pie, lemon tart, lemonade, you name it. If it had lemons in it, it was for here. This is her lemon pound cake recipe

Ingredients
- 3 1/4 cups All-Purpose Flour
- 1/2 teaspoon salt
- 1 1/2 cups butter, softened
- 1 (8 oz.) package of cream cheese, softened
- 3 cups sugar
- 6 large eggs, at room temp
- 1 teaspoon lemon extract
- 1/2 teaspoon vanilla
- Juice of 1 lemon plus zest

Instructions

1. Heat oven to 325°F. Coat 10-inch tube pan with flour no-stick cooking spray.

2.   Combine flour and salt in small bowl; set aside. Beat butter and cream cheese with electric mixer about 60 seconds or until smooth. Add sugar gradually; beat on medium-high speed 5 minutes or until mixture is light and fluffy.

3.   Beat in eggs, one at a time, beating well after each addition. Stir in vanilla, lemon extract, lemon juice and zest. Fold in flour just until combined (do not overmix). Spoon batter into prepared pan.

4.   Bake 1 hour 20 minutes to 1 hour 30 minutes or until a toothpick inserted in center comes out clean. Cool in pan on cooling rack 15 minutes. Remove from pan. Cool completely on cooling rack.

IN THE LAND OF PLASTIC FLOWERS

The beauty of this world can make me sad sometimes,
because I know that I shall not partake of it for long.
You see, life is a fleeting vapor, yes, a mist, that at its
syrupiest disappears and is gone seemingly forever.

When my time here ends, they'll lay my old, tired body down.
I'm going to a better place, but where it lies there are no
flowers.
Nor are there lazy mountain streams to carry my thoughts
away.
Yes, Heaven is beautiful I've been told, and I do believe it's so.

When I've gone, the sun will still come up over the Marshes.
of Glynn, setting them golden and afire with its light.
The sun will still slowly traverse the width of this great land,
and
Finally drop from view into the Pacific Ocean off Monterey.

People will still stand at Glacier Point at sunset, and watch
the pink alpenglow dance along the crest of the Sierra Nevada.
The memory of this ethereal sight still takes my breath away.
I shall truly miss it, I suppose, but it will not remember me.

The legacy I leave will be in my son, other family, and friends.
Those whom I have loved and served as best I could down here.

That will have to be beauty enough for me because I know
there are only faded plastic flowers in the place where I will lie.

JUST A PART OF ONE CENTERVILLE FAMILY'S STORY

My 3rd great grandfather on Dad's side was a man named Richard Holt. Richard was a character. Richard's father came from England and settled in Virginia around 1775. Richard was born in 1796 and came to Gwinnett County in 1819 when he was 23 years old. He settled in Rockbridge District on Yellow River near the old Ballard Mill. All this was before the land lottery. He took a job as a drayman, driving a 4 horse wagon. He hauled and delivered goods between Augusta and Gibraltar (Stone Mountain). It was during his drayman days that he met his wife, Mahala Paschall. Mahala had a nice dowry of $1000. With the dowry money Richard bought the old Ballard Mill and went into the milling business. He was successful for a while, but eventually got deep in debt. He sold the mill to his friend, Thomas Maguire who renamed it Annes Mill in honor of his daughter. Richard turned the rest of his property over to his creditors. He was flat broke, or so he thought. Then he remembered he still had one sheep somewhere in the woods near his house. He borrowed a horse and a gun from his friend, Elijah Anderson, and spent two days looking for that sheep. When he finally found it he shot it. The story goes, that he rode back to Anderson's house, Pleasant Valley. Elijah met him and asked why he'd killed his last sheep. Richard replied, "If I have to start over, I want to start over with nothing." He did start over and succeeded in accumulating a small fortune. The 1850 census shows that he owned 15 slaves. The 1860 tax digest shows that he owned 882 acres of farmland in Gwinnett County. He was a member of Rockbridge Baptist Church. He and Mahala had 15 children. The Holt Family Bible recorded his passing thusly, "Richard Holt was taken sick on Monday the 18th of August and died on the 25th 1862." He was buried in the Stone Mountain City Cemetery. Mahala outlived him by 16 years, passing in 1878. She's buried in the Holt-Juhan Cemetery in Centerville.

Richard Nathaniel Holt Sr 1796-1862
3rd great-grandfather

Eliza Holt Juhan 1819-1903
Daughter of Richard Nathaniel Holt Sr

Savannah Susie (Flossie) Juhan Freeman 1859-1920
Daughter of Eliza Holt Juhan

Nathaniel Sephus Freeman 1888-1970
Son of Savannah Susie (Flossie) Juhan Freeman

Nathaniel Morris Freeman 1930-2019
Son of Nathaniel Sephus Freeman

Terry Robert Freeman
You are the son of Nathaniel Morris Freeman

The little chart above shows my connection to Richard Holt.

John Freeman and his wife Mimmie came to Centerville from Morgan County in the late 1820's. They're my 3rd great grandparents. John and Mimmie had 8 boys. Their first son John T. Jr. arrived in 1829. In 1831 Josephus made his appearance, followed by James in 1833. After James came William in 1835 followed by Leroy in October of 1836. Dudley arrived close behind in 1837. George Washington was born in 1841. And finally, Hamilton Franklin, their surprise came along in July of 1847. I wish this story had a happy ending, but it doesn't.

The Civil War started in 1861 and brought tragedy and heartache to the Freemans and thousands of other families in the North and South. Let's see what happened to the boys. I'll go in their order of enlistment.

Dudley had moved to Mississippi. In March of 1861 he joined the 14th Mississippi Infantry Regiment (Beauregard Rifles). Also, in March of 1862 Leroy, and George Washington joined the 42nd Georgia Infantry Regiment, Company B (Gwinnett County Rebels). In May of 1862, James followed his brothers into the 42nd Georgia Infantry Regiment, Company B (Gwinnett County Rebels). John, also in May of 1862 enlisted in 55th Georgia Infantry Regiment, Company I.

In September of 1862 my 2nd great grandfather, Josephus, went all the way to Canton, Georgia to join the 35th Georgia Infantry Regiment, Company F. Why all the way to Canton, some 61 miles as the crow flies? Well, Josephus' best friend, George Allen Campbell (also my 2nd great grandfather) had joined the 35th Georgia when they were recruiting in Gwinnett County. He wanted to be with his friend. The 35th Georgia was part of Thomas' Brigade, A. P. Hill's Division, Thomas "Stonewall" Jackson's 2nd Corps. He "saw the elephant" (slang for a man's first battle) at Fredericksburg Virginia. Joseph's unit took part in the flank attack of Meade's Division. They charged out of their trenches, ran about a mile, performed a perfect wheel-right, and drove Meade's troops back across the Rappahannock.

The picture marks where the 35th Georgia stopped Meade's advance and drove them back. After the battle Jackson's troops wintered at Camp Gregg. Camp Gregg was about 8 miles south of Fredericksburg, 8 miles east of Guinea Station, and about 2 miles west of the Rappahannock. Elizabeth's application for a widow's pension indicates, through eyewitness affidavit, he died of "Brain Fever". The mid-1800's name for meningitis. That ended enlistments of the Freeman boys, for a while at least.

While the war was raging, and men were dying, some good things happened too. Josephus and his wife Elizabeth had a daughter, Sarah. George Washington and his wife Alice had a baby girl, May Oma. James and his wife Elizabeth had a daughter, Neaty Carolyn. All these precious girls were born in 1862, and I'm sure brought joy to the Freeman family. This joy was short lived.

They lost Dudley first, but more about that later. In early June of 1863 their worst fears were realized. As we saw earlier, Josephus died in May 1863. They received word of his death in June. Two months later they received news that George Washington was killed in a skirmish outside Montgomery, Alabama. Then, two months after that they were notified that their oldest boy, John, was taken prisoner at Cumberland Gap, Tennessee. John ended up in the infamous Union POW prison, Camp Douglas. You've probably never heard of Camp Douglas, or any of the other Union POW camps. Some were better than others, but Camp Douglas was every bit as horrible as Andersonville. John would die there of smallpox in 1864. He lies in a mass grave in Oak Woods Cemetery in Chicago with over 6,000 other men. That grave is called Confederate Mound.

The monument at Confederate Mound

Now, let's go back and look at Dudley. Dudley enlisted on March 28, 1861, in Corinth, Mississippi for the term of one year. He didn't make his year out. Dudley was killed on February 12, 1862, in a skirmish before the Battle of Fort Donelson. Like many men in the Confederate army Dudley wasn't paid regularly. In fact, he drew his last pay on September 1, 1861.

One day Josephus' father-in-law, Jesse Bryan (also my 3rd great grandfather), was visiting with John and Mimmie. Mr. Bryan asked John if he had applied for Dudley's back pay. John said no, he didn't know he could. So, with Mr. Bryan's help, John applied for Dudley's back pay on June 19th, 1862. They had to go to Covington, Georgia to make the application. His petition was approved, and he was paid $88.40 on June 21st. $88.40 for a son. This scenario was played out hundreds of times across the South. The Union boy's parents had a little easier time getting their son's back pay, but like their Southern counterparts, they'd rather have had their boys.

Elizabeth never remarried after Josephus' death. She lived out her life in their home on Campbell Road in Centerville.

Josephus and Elizabeth Freeman's House 1976

She is mentioned in Thomas McGuire's farm" diary as among the women who knitted socks for Confederate soldiers. According to her grandson, Nathaniel S. Freeman, she was a fearless woman. He told of her living alone in the last house on a lonely road. She kept a gun by her bed and a jug of corn whiskey under it. Probably some of her son A. D.'s corn "likker" if I had to bet. She took a sip of the corn whiskey every night before she went to sleep. If she heard a noise in the night she'd get up, light her lamp, get her gun, and go outside to see who or what it was. A pioneer woman for sure!

The 35th Georgia was with Lee's Army of Northern Virginia when the end came at Appomattox Courthouse in April 1865. The regiment surrendered 15 officers and 121 men. At that time, they were under the command of Colonel Bolling H. Holt. Among those 121 ragged, starving soldiers was Josephus' friend, and my 2nd great grandfather, George Allen Campbell. General Grant was kind enough to feed the remnants of Lee's army.

The picture shows the condition of Southern soldiers after the surrender. George surrendered his arms, filled his belly, and set out walking the 385 miles home to Centerville. Like most men his shoes were rotten, and by the time he'd walked a few miles, they were gone. Early April in Virginia in those days was cold and it snowed frequently. It must have been a miserable walk, but at least no one was shooting at him. He was finally going home.

My family's post-Civil War struggle was the rule, not the exception. Life after the war was hard. Not to say that their lives before the war was a bed of roses. Their world was turned upside down. Friends and family lay "moldering in the grave" as the song says.

NANNY PAT'S PECAN PIE

Is this a "pee-can" pie, or a "puh-can" pie? Yes. It's both, depending on where in the South you're from. No matter how you pronounce it this pecan pie is great. Nanny Pat made one or two of every Thanksgiving.

Ingredients

Dough:

- 1 1/4 cups all-purpose flour
- 2 teaspoons sugar
- 1/8 teaspoon salt
- 1/2 cup cold butter (1 stick), diced
- 1 large egg, lightly beaten
- Flour, for rolling the dough

Filling:

- 5 tablespoons unsalted butter
- 1 cup packed light brown sugar
- 3/4 cup light corn syrup

- 1/2 teaspoon fine salt
- 2 cups chopped toasted pecans
- 1 to 2 tablespoons bourbon
- 2 teaspoons pure vanilla extract3 eggs, lightly beaten

Instructions

1. You gotta make the dough by hand: In a medium bowl, whisk together the flour, sugar, and salt. Using your fingers, work the butter into the dry ingredients until it resembles yellow cornmeal mixed with bean-sized bits of butter. (If the flour/butter mixture gets warm, refrigerate it for 10 minutes before proceeding.) Add the egg and stir the dough together with a fork or by hand in the bowl. If the dough is dry, sprinkle up to a tablespoon more of cold water over the mixture.
2. Cheaters can make the dough in a food processor. With the machine fitted with the metal blade, pulse the flour, sugar, and salt until combined. Add the butter and pulse until it resembles yellow cornmeal mixed with bean-sized bits of butter, about 10 times. Add the egg and pulse 1 to 2 times; don't let the dough form into a ball in the machine. (If the dough is very dry add up to a tablespoon more of cold water.) Remove the bowl from the machine, remove the blade, and bring the dough together by hand.
3. Form the dough into a disk, wrap with plastic wrap, and refrigerate until thoroughly chilled, at least 1 hour.
4. On a lightly floured surface, roll the dough with a rolling pin into a 12-inch circle about 1/8-inch thick. Transfer the dough to a 9-inch pie pan and trim the edges, leaving about an extra

inch hanging over the edge. Tuck the overhanging dough underneath itself to form a thick edge that is even with the rim. Flute the edge as desired. Freeze the pie shell for 30 minutes.

5. Set separate racks in the center and lower third of oven and preheat to 400 degrees F. Put a piece of parchment paper or foil over the pie shell and fill with dried beans or pie weights. Bake on a baking sheet on the center rack until the dough is set, about 20 minutes. Remove from the oven and lift sides of the parchment paper to remove the beans. Continue baking until the pie shell is lightly golden brown, about 10 more minutes. Reduce the oven temperature to 350 degrees Fahrenheit.

6. While the crust is baking make the filling: In medium saucepan, combine the butter, brown sugar, corn syrup, and salt. Bring to a boil over medium heat, and stirring constantly, continue to boil for 1 minute. Remove from the heat and stir in the nuts, bourbon, and the vanilla. Set the mixture aside to cool slightly, about 5 minutes. (If the crust has cooled, return it to the oven for 5 minutes to warm through.) Whisk the beaten eggs into the filling until smooth. Put the pie shell on a sheet pan and pour the filling into the hot crust.

7. Bake on the lower oven rack until the edges are set but the center is still slightly loose, about 40 to 45 minutes. (If the edges get very dark, cover them with aluminum foil halfway during baking.) Cool on a rack. Serve slightly warm or room temperature.

As with any Freeman made, served warm pie, it's always permissible, yea required, to serve with a scoop of vanilla ice cream. It makes it more decadent than it already is. Enjoy!

A TRUE CHRISTIAN (FOR MY FRIEND, BILL MENG)

True Christianity is more than stained glass windows and dark wood.
It's a deeply centered principle that drives everything we strive to be.
I've known many "Christians" who didn't really know where they stood.
So deep in bondage to laws and expectations, unable to break free.

Pomp and circumstance are just that and nothing more,
and talk is cheap and meaningless if the life you live isn't true.
To learn to walk in peace and let our spirits on wings of eagle's soar,
is the essence of God's truth and should guide everything we do.

Occasionally, in this world you find someone who's true to the end.
A person who quietly lives their Christianity for all the world to see.
I knew a man like that, and I'm honored to have called him a friend.
His quiet, but powerful witness remains an inspiration to me.

I watched him live his faith in the greatest of life's trials.

When his integrity, honor, and ability were questioned by many.
Through all the heartache and pain, he kept silent and smiled.
And though he wrestled with our enemy, bitterness, I never saw any.

He focused on the important things of life like his family and his God.
When the storm was raging, he stood calmly grinning at apparent disaster.
His detractors couldn't or wouldn't understand and thought him odd.
He uttered not a word and refused to let their attacks become his master.

If true success is found in the life lived measured against words spoken,
and a winner defined by the number of people he touches, not races won,
then he was both, faith sustained him until he left us too soon but unbroken.
Bill Meng, a true Christian, remembered by love given away and things done.

BONUS RECIPES

Granny Freeman's Real Banana Pudding

This desert was my favorite growing up. Probably because it was only served on special occasions. Papa Freeman said if you set a bowl of Granny Freeman's Banana Pudding on your forehead your tongue would slap you brains out trying to get it. I never tried it, but I'm sure he was right. Have I ever told you I wore Husky size pants when I was a boy?

Ingredients

- 1/2 cup sugar
- 2 tablespoons cornstarch
- 1 teaspoon salt
- 2 1/4 cups whole milk
- 4 large eggs, separated
- 2 tablespoons unsalted butter
- 1 teaspoon vanilla extract
- 3 1/3 cups vanilla wafers
- 4 ripe bananas, cut into 1/2" slices
- 3 tablespoons sugar

Instructions

1. Preheat oven to 375°F. Whisk together first 3 ingredients in a small bowl. Whisk together sugar

mixture, milk, and 4 egg yolks in a medium-size heavy saucepan until well blended. Cook over medium heat, stirring constantly, 6 to 8 minutes or until thickened. Remove from heat; stir in butter and vanilla.

2. Layer half of vanilla wafers in an 8-inch square baking dish. Top with half of banana slices and half of pudding. Repeat procedure with remaining wafers, banana slices, and pudding.

3. Beat egg whites at high speed with an electric mixer until foamy. Gradually add 3 Tbsp. sugar, beating until sugar dissolves and stiff peaks form, about 5 minutes. Spread meringue over pudding, sealing to edge of dish.

4. Bake at 375°F for 7 to 9 minutes or until golden. Let cool 30 minutes, and serve warm; or chill an additional hour, and serve cold.

Tip: Pudding gets thicker as it cools. When warm, it may be a bit looser.

Mama's Sweet Potato Souffle

Like Mama's Candied Yams this Sweet Potato Souffle is a rich side dish that makes a great dessert. You might need a backrub or a nap after eating this.

Ingredients

- 1 pound Sweet Potatoes
- 1 teaspoon Vanilla
- Nutmeg & Cinnamon, to taste
- 2 Eggs, beaten
- 4 tablespoons salted Butter, soft
- Evaporated Milk
- 6 tablespoons Sugar
- 2 cups miniature Marshmallows

Instructions

1. In a stock pot, boil sweet potatoes on medium-high.

2. Simmer for one hour, until soft.

3. Drain and cool.

4. Peel potatoes and mash them in a large mixing bowl.

5. Preheat oven to 350.

6. Prepare a baking dish with butter.

7. Add remaining ingredients (except Eggs & Marshmallows) to sweet potatoes.

8. Mix eggs and add more sugar if desired.

9. Pour into baking dish, baking about 30-40 minutes.

10. Heat oven to 475.

11. Spread marshmallows on souffle, baking about five minutes until browned.

Terry's Tater Tot Casserole

This recipe is so easy to make and tasty too. I love tater tots, but who doesn't.

Ingredients

- 1 pound ground beef
- 1 pinch garlic powder
- salt and pepper to taste
- 1 cup chopped onion
- 1 (8 ounce) package shredded cheddar cheese
- 1 (32 ounce) package tater tots, thawed
- 1 (10.75 ounce) can condensed cream of mushroom soup
- 1 (10.75 ounce) can condensed cream of celery soup
- 1 (10.75 ounce) can milk
- 1 pinch garlic powder

Instructions

1. Preheat the oven to 375 degrees F.
2. Cook ground beef and onions until beef is done and onions are clear.
3. Spread beef and onion mixture in a 9x13-inch baking pan, sprinkle mixture with garlic powder, salt, and pepper. Cover with tater tots.

4. In a bowl, stir together mushroom soup, celery soup, and milk. Pour the soup mixture over the tater tots and beef and sprinkle with additional garlic powder.
5. Sprinkle cheese on top.
6. Bake in preheated oven for 60 minutes, or until cheese is melted and slightly brown and casserole is bubbling.

BONUS POEMS

Snowin' on Persimmon

I had a gal
She was my life
I knew she would make a fine wife
I couldn't know
I wouldn't see
She'd never take any time for me

Now it's
Snowin' on Persimmon
Big ole flakes are tumbling down
Yes, it's
Snowin' on Persimmon
And my baby can't be found

It was Spring
Now it's Winter
It was Fall when she disappeared
I looked high
I looked low
But she was gone just as I feared

Now it's
Snowin' on Persimmon
Big ole flakes are tumbling down
Yes, it's
Snowin' on Persimmon
And my baby can't be found

Day is short
Life is long
And life without her ain't no life at all
I was blind
But now I see
My heart is broke, but I'm not free

Now it's

Snowin' on Persimmon
Big ole flakes are tumbling down
Yes it's
Snowin' on Persimmon
And my baby can't be found

I love Bluegrass music. This is my attempt at the lyrics for a Bluegrass song.

The Irony of It

I see things in black and white.
You see them in shades of gray,
as somewhat defined objects dancing in the mist.
Both of us are right and that's the irony of it.
Talk is cheap when it's not from the heart.
Communication fades to black,
and with it any hope of understanding.
Both of us are wrong and that's the irony of it.
Sometimes this dilemma causes us pain.
The anger ebbs and flows like the sea
as it laps against our emotions.
Both of us are hurt and that's the irony of it.
The longer we're together the closer we get.
The paradox of it all is astounding.
The very things that separate also bind.
Both of us are in love and that's the irony of it.

The Unknowns

I walked on hallowed ground today.
It'd been a while since I'd passed that way.
The tombstones at attention; tall and white
as the failing day gave way to the night.

I stood quietly near the unknown's tomb,
and wondered who lay in its cold, dark womb.
Awaiting that great and glorious day
when the dead shall rise and be on their way.

Did his mother weep a mournful tear
when she realized her worst fear?
Did she lie awake in her bed,
and weep for her boy that was dead?

Did he have a wife and family?
Was his dying thought to with her be?
Did he long to lay his head on her breast
as the specter of death stole away his breath?

I stood there lost in my thoughts
of these unknown souls and the terrible cost.
It was dark as my mood as I walked away.
Good men dead. There was nothing to say.

Not Alone

A storm was moving in fast from the West.
The sky turned as yellow as a daffodil bloom.
An eerie silence fell over the land like a blanket, and I was
alone.

Wind began to blow with a cool breath.
Leaves swirled and danced at its command.
Rain began to fall slowly at first and then in buckets, and I was
alone

Limbs broke loose and crashed to the ground.
Twigs swirled free and scratched my face.
The sky turned as black and foreboding as death, and I was
alone.

Then came hail and the ground was white.
The wind blew stronger and began to moan.
Then thunder boomed and lightening flashed, and I was alone.

Just as suddenly the sky grew brighter.
The cold rain slowed to a drizzle.
A rainbow appeared in the eastern sky, and I know I'm not
alone.

Habitations of Dragons

I know the habitations of dragons.
The dark and dank cairns where they dwell.
I've been to their deepest caverns
where the Know-Light never penetrates.
I have lain down and slept there, not fearing the darkness or
their sulfurous heavy breathing.
I have no fear of dragons
for I know the Dragon Slayer.
He is my friend, and I am His bondservant.
The dragon's fire may scorch my flesh, but I'll not burn.
The sweet potions He applies bring healing.
No, I've never seen the Dragon Slayer,
but I know He is here in me, and that's enough for now.
It won't be long until I see Him.
When I do, the dragons will be gone forever.
Forever.

EPILOGUE

The journey of writing this book started in the summer of 2016. It was just a concept then, an idea, if you will. The thought had been rolling around in my brain for a long time before that, but 2016 is when it began to coagulate. I even started to write some thoughts down.

Judy and I were visiting Mom and Dad in November 2016 when everything changed. Dad and I were working in his shop just before lunch. We were teasing each other about the number of hammers and screwdrivers we had. I had my back to him sorting screws and bolts when I heard a thud. When I turned around Dad was flat on his back struggling to get up. I helped him up and got him in a chair. He'd had a stroke. That started 2 and one-half years of caretaking. He passed away on August 19, 2019.

We still had our house in the mountains but were rarely able to go. It was on Airbnb for a couple of years, but that was a lot of work, and Mom began to decline. By July 2021 we'd had enough, sold the house, and settled in for a long haul of continued caretaking. You see, Mom was in OK health when Dad died, but that changed quickly. She started going in and out of Afib. In the process of trying to bring that to heal we discovered she had a bad heart valve. On top of all that she'd developed pulmonary hypertension. She decided to have the valve job and was beginning to get all the tests for that, and she fell. When she fell, it broke her femur. That was in November of 2020. All those medical problems coupled with the broken leg was the beginning of the end for her. When she got out of the hospital and rehabilitation, she decided not to have the valve replaced. Soon after that decision, she needed 24/7 care. As I said, we sold the mountain house the first part of July. Mom passed away peacefully on July 21. She was sitting in her recliner watching Wendy Williams when she slipped away.

Almost 6 years of around the clock caring for folks, even though you love them, takes its toll. Judy and were both fried mentally, and physically. We just wanted to rest and get to know each other again. So, we did. I could hardly think, much less focus enough to write. Then in early 2022 we found out that Judy had to have major surgery on her neck. It was done on April 15, 2022. So, I restarted my caretaking mentality. That went smooth as could be expected but was draining for both of us. However, with God's help we made it through.

Fast forward to the end of May 2023. I was sitting in my office when the idea for Dust From a Red Dust Road popped back into my head. I sat staring at my computer for a long while, and then just started writing. I've written 4 to 6 hours a day ever since. I'm now at the end of this exercise. It's been exhilarating. Sometimes I can't type fast enough.

I will say one last thing about Centerville. The village of my memories is no longer there. It's been paved over, torn down, and rebuilt a couple of times since my childhood. The fields I worked and played in are subdivisions and strip malls. Mr. Johnson's watermelon patch is a super Wal-Mart. Annistown Falls is no longer visible from Annistown Road. The old one lane steel bridge has been torn down. In its place is a 4-lane concrete bridge. Heck, Annistown Road is 4-lane from Centerville to U.S. 78. The old Rockbridge Trail (now GA 124) is 4-laned too, from Interstate 20 in Lithonia all the way to Lawrenceville, some 24 miles. You can't see the Rock Bridge from GA 124 either. The red dirt roads and white framed farmhouses are all gone. To quote the late John Prine, "they wrote it all down to the progress of man."

I'll close with the old MYF (Methodist Youth Fellowship) benediction: "May the Lord bless you and keep you; may He turn His face toward you and give you peace. Amen"

ACKNOWLEDGEMENTS

I couldn't have done this without my wife Judy's support. She's been my encourager, my first draft editor, the corrector of my rabbit chasing tendencies, and a sounding board for my sometimes crazy ideas. Honest feedback is her forte, and I'll never be able to properly express my appreciation to her. Thanks Babe.

My dear friend, Gail Allgood, has read every word. She's a fantastic writer herself, and if I'm honest her skill intimidates me a little bit. She always has a kind word, and a gentle correction when I use the wrong word. Like the time I wrote "bias-relief" instead of "bas-relief" when describing the carving on Stone Mountain. Thank you, Gail, for all your encouragement and all the great meals over the years.

My son Nathaniel has walked along side me while I wrote this book. He always had a word of encouragement, or a swift kick in the kiester if I needed one. Thanks Nate.

My life long, or so it seems, friend Harold Holcombe. You're a good listener brother. Thanks for taking the time to read the early draft.

Thanks to the men in the Men's Fellowship at Zoar. Y'all let me read my true story, Church Flatulence, and some of you even laughed at the appropriate spots.

Thanks to my editor and friend, Marj Irish. Through the miracle of the Internet, you were able to fix my broken things while living in Australia. Love you kiddo!

Thanks again "Pap" Ewing. I owe you a meal.

Finally, thanks to you dear reader. Your time is valuable. I appreciate you giving a little bit of it to this book. I am humbled.

Final Note:

I'm at the age where loss is becoming a part of life. I'm losing my hair. I've lost weight. I'm losing my balance, and on it goes. The hardest losses are the losing loved ones and friends. Sometimes they are one and the same. Both of my parents have crossed over, and their brothers and sisters, my uncles and aunts have too. So have friends like Rick Caldwell, Steve Jones, Max Watts, Bill Meng, Doug Franklin, Kathy Cerveny, Joan Musser (The Reverend Mother) and Ken Carnegie.

Right before publication I lost two of those friends who were also loved ones: Bob Bramblett, and Thomas Livsey. Rest easy my brothers. I'll see you soon.

BOOKS BY THIS AUTHOR

Rebel Soldiers, And Other Musings On The Vanity Of Life

A book of poetry.

www.ingramcontent.com/pod-product-compliance
Lightning Source LLC
Chambersburg PA
CBHW021135090426
42740CB00008B/791